Glacier Country
MONTANA'S GLACIER NATIONAL PARK

by R.C. "Bert" Gildart and others

Number 4; Revised

Montana Magazine
American Geographic Publishing
Helena, Montana

ISBN 0-938314-38-6

© 1990 American Geographic Publishing
P.O. Box 5630, Helena, MT 59604
(406) 443-2842

William A. Cordingley, Chairman
Rick Graetz, President & CEO
Mark O. Thompson, Director of Publications
Barbara Fifer, Production Manager
Linda Collins, Graphic Artist

Photography edited by John Reddy

Design by Len Visual Design
Printed in Hong Kong by
    Nordica International Ltd.

American Geographic Publishing is a corporation for publishing illustrated geographic information and guides. It is not associated with American Geographical Society. It has no commercial or legal relationship to and should not be confused with any other company, society or group using the words geographic or geographical in its name or its publications.

Library of Congress Cataloging-in-Publication Data
Glacier country : Montana's Glacier National Park. -- Rev. ed. / by Robert C. Gildart and others.
    p.   cm. -- (Montana geographic series ; no. 4)
    ISBN 0-938314-38-6 : $13.95
    1. Geology--Montana--Glacier National Park. 2. Natural history--Montana--Glacier National Park. 3. Glacier National Park (Mont.)--History. 4. Glacier National Park (Mont.) I. Gildart, Robert C. II. Series
QE 134.G57G53   1990
978.6'52--dc20
                                            90-385
                                            CIP

GLACIER NATIONAL PARK

MONTANA TOPOGRAPHIC MAP PORTION REPRODUCED FROM MONTANA STATE WALL MAP. © RAVEN MAPS & IMAGES, (800) 237-0798.

Contents

Left: Lake McDonald on a September afternoon.
Facing page: A browsing mule deer buck at sunset.

Title page: Cracker Lake from the summit of Siyeh Mountain.
DOUG DYE

Front cover: Mt. Gould from Swiftcurrent Lake. LARRY ULRICH

Back cover, top left: Indian paintbrush, Lewis's monkeyflower
and arnica on Logan Pass. LARRY ULRICH
Top right: McDonald Creek. WERNER STEBNER
Bottom: Ptarmigan. CONRAD ROWE

JEFF GNASS

Introduction

by R.C. "Bert" Gildart

Glacier National Park can be approached from all four points of the compass, but the eastern approach is the one that is particularly inspiring. From this direction, along Highway 2 through the flatlands of North Dakota and Montana, there is little hint of the vast mountainous range that looms ahead. Not until you are about 50 miles away, and suddenly ascend from the depths of a coulee, is there any real assurance that what appeared to be high glimmering clouds is in fact a lofty range of mountains shrouded in snow and ice.

Some 230 years ago, when this range was first seen by whites, adventurers were prompted to call this the "land of shining mountains." Today, this area could be called the land of glorious adversity, for contemporary scientists tell us that the park was born of fire, quenched by torrential rains, inundated by vast seas, forced upward by internal pressures, and then gouged by great continental ice sheets that came and went on at least four occasions. From this heritage, mountains were molded that reach up to touch the sky and cradle more than 200 lakes. Such is the legacy the eons left for some 60 species mammals, 200 of birds and 1,200 of plants that now inhabit the 1,538 square miles of Glacier National Park.

Glacier's features can be enjoyed with drink in hand from a recliner on the terrace of one of the park's four magnificent lodges, from the deck of a launch, by bus, by car or by foot. Personal tastes determine how to spend the time, and so it is advisable to become acquainted with the park's generalized features as quickly as possible. The Park Service is prepared to assist in a number of ways.

Near each entrance is either an information center or an elaborate visitor center. Here, rangers and naturalists are available to acquaint travelers with the various types of accommodations and interpretive programs. In addition, displays assist interpretation and guide the curious to places of interest.

At first encounter, the park may appear a forbidding place to explore, but this is not the case. It is bisected by the famed Going-To-The-Sun Road, which provides motorists with numerous pullovers for introductions to various features. Guided tour buses, provided by park concessionaires, relieve motorists of driving.

After this introductory tour many visitors are inspired to explore on foot. Almost 700 miles of trails await the hiker, extending from low forested hills up to boulder-strewn passes. Reached by several of these trails, two back-country chalets cater to hikers who do not want to carry heavy packs. In fact, it isn't necessary to tote anything more than bear bells, a toothbrush, camera, a canteen of water and a map, as both Granite and Sperry chalets provide food and bedding.

Remote campgrounds provide hikers with nature's own accommodations. As in many other parks, these sites now require reservations made only in person at the park and on a first-come, first-serve basis.

Glacier is a park of incredible natural diversity. Five habitat types occur here, largely determined by weather, which in turn is influenced by altitude. In Glacier, then, it is possible to see grassland, deciduous forest, coniferous forest, alpine tundra, and even the equivalent of polar ice and snow. The habitat changes visitors witness as they rise through Glacier's elevations equals what they would see driving thousands of miles north across the United States and Canada.

For those interested in learning about wildlife and the areas where it can be found, it is advisable to learn Glacier's zones. In the spring, for instance, the initiated go to the coniferous forest to find elk, moose, squirrels and chipmunks, and the most cooperative and photogenic blue grouse. Follow the bird's ventriloquistic hooting to its territory to observe the display of roseate shoulder patches and flaring eye patch as it warns other grouse away.

Perhaps Glacier's most spectacular zone is the arctic-alpine. Here, hardy wildflowers have adapted to this harsh climate in a variety of ways. Some of the flowers are covered with fine hair-like structures that retard evaporation from the desiccating winds. Other plants have overcome these forces by growing in mats and clumps. Almost all are perennials; the short alpine summer doesn't allow enough time for annuals to complete their life cycles.

Despite the adverse conditions of the arctic-alpine zone, this area is home for some of the park's most interesting wildlife. Sheep may be seen in a variety of locales, but one particularly good spot is midway between Logan Pass and Granite Park Chalet. Interested visitors should leave Logan Pass and hike the Garden Wall Trail. Four miles along, a huge formation juts away from the main ridge of mountains like a flying buttress. This monolith is Haystack Butte; here, in its bracing arch, snow lingers and provides sheep, as well as goats and marmots, with a cool reprieve from the intense alpine sun. July through September is the best time to visit this area as, with the advent of cool weather, all but a few specially adapted species (such as the ptarmigan) either migrate from the arctic-alpine area or hibernate beneath Glacier's inevitable mantle of snow.

This book is an introduction to the general landscape, colorful past and natural diversity of Glacier National Park, which many Americans think of first when they envision Montana.

ERWIN & PEGGY BAUER

Above: Bald eagle.

Facing page: *Bearhat Mountain as seen from Hidden Lake Pass.*

Glaciated Park

Facing page: Lake McDonald.

by Dave Alt

Glacier Park. It should have been called "Glaciated Park," because this is a poor place to see modern glaciers, and an excellent place to see mountains sculpted by the great ice-age glaciers.

And an excellent place to see many other things.

Those mountains consist of sedimentary rocks more than 1 billion years old, some of the oldest well preserved sedimentary rocks in the country. The rocks preserve a record of the earth as it was before land plants existed, before there were animals of any kind, or atmospheric oxygen that animals might breathe. The record tells of a planet so unfamiliar that it might be another planet, as distant in space as in time.

So 60 million or so years ago, those rocks moved into their present position during the crustal movements that created the Rocky Mountains. Evidence of that movement is clearly visible in the landscape of the eastern part of Glacier Park.

During the last 2 or 3 million years, a succession of great ice ages brought enormous glaciers to North America and northern Europe, and to high mountains all over the world. At least during the last ice age, and presumably during earlier ice ages, an ice cap covered the high areas of Glacier Park, and huge rivers of ice creaked awkwardly down the large canyons, scouring the bedrock and then dumping their loads of eroded sediment farther down the valley.

The grinding rivers of ice melted about 10,000 years ago, leaving their legacy in the craggy peaks and ridges, the deep valleys and the sparkling lakes that make the modern landscape of Glacier Park so magnificently beautiful. Only glaciation on a large scale can bring mountains to such rugged perfection.

THE ARCHIVES OF A VANISHED PLANET

Almost all the rocks exposed in the cliffs and roadcuts of Glacier Park began as layers of sand, mud and lime mud deposited a billion or more years ago. Now they are layers of sandstone, mudstone and limestone. Most of the rocks in the park date from an extremely long interval that geologists call Precambrian time, because it preceded the Cambrian period when the first animals appeared on earth.

A billion years is a long time, even by the elongated standards of geology, and the Precambrian formations in Glacier Park rank among the oldest well preserved sedimentary rocks in the country. Like all sedimentary rocks, they contain a record of the environment in which the original sand and mud accumulated. The Precambrian rocks in Glacier Park appear to have formed in an environment unlike any that exists today, unlike any that has existed for hundreds of millions of years. The earth of a billion years ago had not yet developed into the pleasant and hospitable home we know.

This is not the place to discuss the subject in detail, but it seems worth mentioning that billion-year-old sedimentary rocks commonly contain evidence of an atmosphere that contained only a trace of oxygen. We would quickly suffocate, if we could visit the earth of that time. Furthermore, the scarcity of atmospheric oxygen would have left the earth without its ozone layer, which now protects the surface from burning ultraviolet radiation.

However, the rocks do provide good reason to suspect that the Precambrian atmosphere did contain enormous amounts of carbon dioxide. Now we pass from the realm of solid observation into that of informed conjecture. If the ancient atmosphere did indeed include large amounts of carbon dioxide, that would have made the climate hot, because carbon dioxide causes a greenhouse effect. High temperatures, if they existed, would have increased the rate of evaporation from the oceans to create an effect that may have resembled a planetary sauna bath.

Picture then the shadeless landscape of Precambrian time. The barren land sweltered under heavy clouds and was lifeless except for scummy growths of green algae in shallow pools of water. The seacoast lay somewhere near Glacier Park, probably shifting back and forth as the years passed. Most of the rocks we see in the park appear to have accumulated near that coast, some on land, others in shallow water not very far from land.

The rock formations of Glacier Park are few in number, very thick, and appear as broad bands of distinctive color in the landscape. Anyone can quickly learn to recognize them. Pebbles eroded from those formations make the brightly colorful stream beds that so many visitors to the park remember long after they forget some of the more spectacular sights.

Looking down on McDonald Valley.

The Appekuny mudstone

The Appekuny mudstone is several thousand feet of somber green rock that becomes very dark in the western part of the park. The formation is more than 3,000 feet thick, and it forms a dark-gray or greenish-gray band in the landscape. At close range, it is simply layered green rock in the eastern part of the park; in the western part, rock so dark that it is almost black. Any green rock in Glacier Park is almost certainly Appekuny mudstone.

At the top of the Appekuny mudstone, layers of red mudstone begin to appear, and they increase in numbers upwards. Geologists draw the contact between the Appekuny mudstone and the Grinnell mudstone above it where the red begins to overwhelm the green.

The Grinnell mudstone

The Grinnell mudstone is about 2,500 feet thick, a broad reddish band in the landscape. Roadcuts of Grinnell mudstone are as red as a freshly painted barn, as they should be, because the same iron oxide pigment colors both. Except in the highest mountains near the middle of the park, any red rock in Glacier Park is likely to be Grinnell mudstone.

Watch the exposures of red mudstone for fossil mudcracks and ripple marks that look as though they were on a modern mudflat at low tide. Similar structures also exist in the green Appekuny formation, although not nearly so abundantly as in the red mudstones. As we look at those ripple marks and mudcracks, we see the remains of rippling pools of shallow water that lay here a billion years ago, and of mudflats that baked hard in the heat. However, geologists cannot be sure whether those pools and mudflats existed near the seashore, along the borders of a desert lake, or perhaps in some obsolete environment that has not existed since Precambrian time.

Both the Appekuny and Grinnell mudstones contain a few beds of white sandstone that make prominent ledges on the hillsides. Some of the most beautiful rock outcrops in the park display bright red Grinnell mudstone and stark white sandstone in vivid contrast.

The Altyn limestone

The oldest Precambrian formation in Glacier Park is the Altyn limestone of the eastern mountain front. It tends to be a bit inconspicuous, even though it is about 2,000 feet thick, and is most easily seen around the Many Glacier Hotel and the east end of St. Mary Lake. Altyn limestone is almost white in fresh roadcuts, tan on weathered surfaces, and contains numerous sand grains and small pebbles. It appears to have accumulated in shallow waters, perhaps in sea water, although there is no way to be quite sure of that. The Altyn limestone passes upward into the green and dark gray mudstones of the Appekuny formation.

The Siyeh limestone

Pale gray cliffs of Siyeh limestone tower above the red Grinnell mudstones to dominate the high country in most of the central part of Glacier Park. The formation is about 3,500 feet thick and, more than any other, is the rock that park visitors see.

Many exposures of Siyeh limestone contain fossil algal structures called "stromatolites" that look almost as though they might be fossil cabbages. Exactly similar structures grow today in a few places, so we know that stromatolites are the remains of extremely primitive blue-green algae. We are all familiar with blue-green algae as the plant that forms scummy growth in puddles, covers the north sides of trees and rocks, and infests fish tanks. Stromatolites range from a few inches to several feet in diameter, and they commonly formed reefs that completely fill entire layers of rock. Some of the ledges of Siyeh limestone around Logan Pass and

PAT O'HARA

KATHY AHLENSLAGER

TOM J. ULRICH

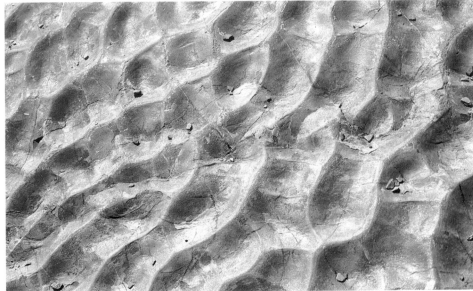

Above: *Ripple marks on Swiftcurrent Peak.*
Near left: *Glacial scratches.*
Far left: *Mudstone design.*

9

JAMES RANDKLEV

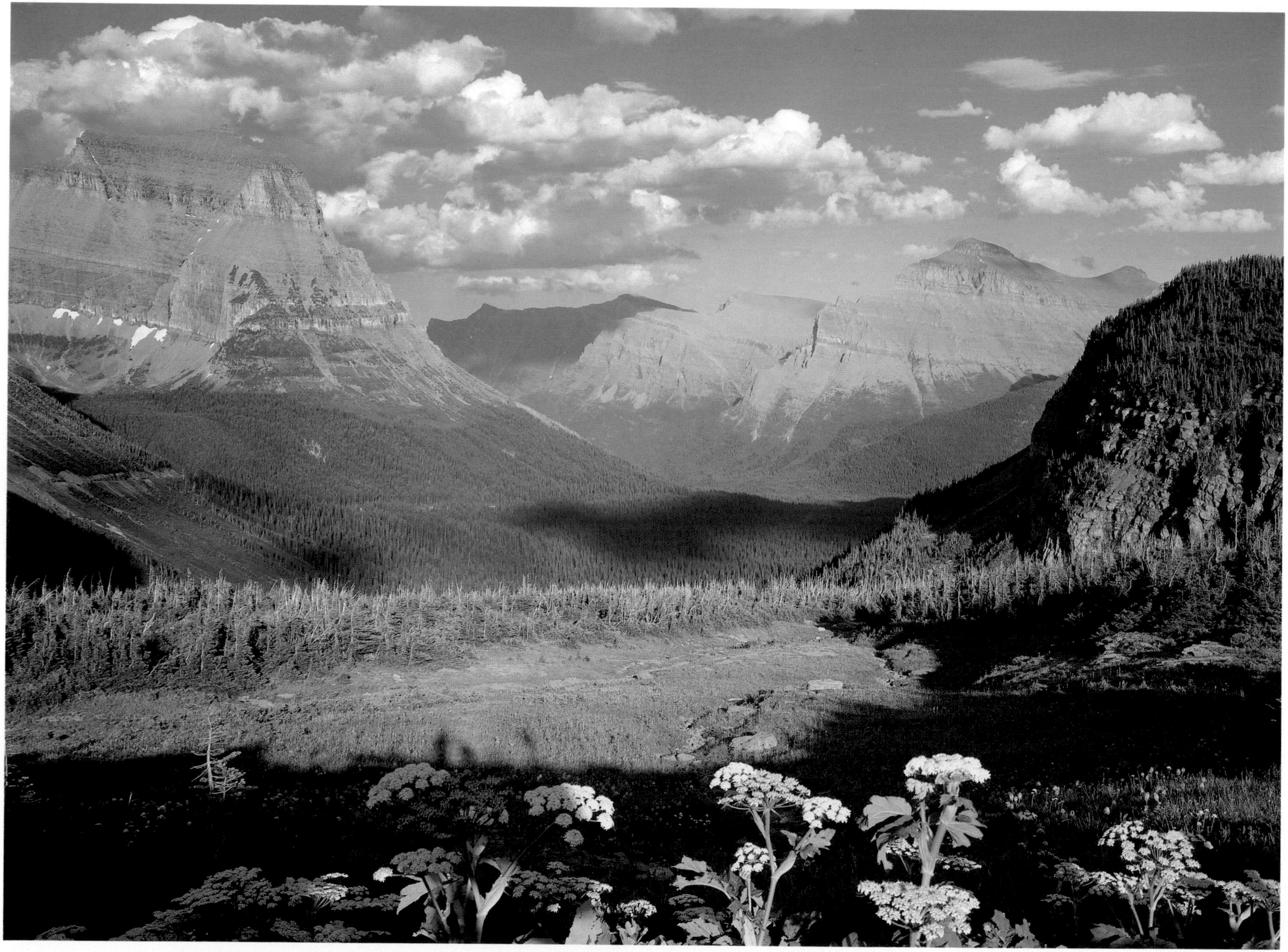

LEE KAISER

JOHN REDDY

along the trail to Hidden Lake contain excellent stromatolites. Similar fossils exist locally and less abundantly in the Altyn limestone and the red mudstones. We should all view those fossils with respect and admiration, as early pioneers that led the way for other forms of life. We would not be here now had they not been here then.

Primitive though they are, blue-green algae are green plants that do absorb atmospheric carbon dioxide, produce organic matter, and release oxygen to create the kind of air animals can breathe.

Of course, an atom of carbon buried in sedimentary rocks must balance every molecule of oxygen in the atmosphere to account for the original carbon dioxide. The Siyeh limestone is dark in fresh exposures because it contains organic matter, so much in some places that freshly broken rock smells putrid. That billion-year-old odor of decay is one of the reasons that the air we breathe contains oxygen.

11

Heat from the magma drove the dark organic stain out of the Siyeh limestone above and below the sill, bleaching it white. So the sill appears as a nearly horizontal black band bordered in white above and below, a conspicuous striped ribbon on many of the cliffs high in the park. Several roadcuts at the top of Logan Pass expose the Purcell sill, and the Logan Pass end of the trail to Granite Park passes several outstanding exposures of the sill, and of the bleached limestone near its borders.

At Granite Park, the Purcell sill turns into a lava flow of the kind that geologists call "pillow basalt." The magma evidently erupted into the water in which the Siyeh limestone was accumulating, and formed a pile of cylindrical masses that look a bit like oversized pillows where we see them exposed in outcrops. Lavas that erupt under water generally do that.

Age dates obtained by analyzing the radioactive elements in diabase from the Purcell sill show that it is slightly more than 1 billion years old. That must also be the age of the upper part of the Siyeh limestone, because the sill erupted as a lava flow into the formation while it was still soft and muddy. Therefore, all the rocks below the Siyeh limestone must be more than 1 billion years old, perhaps much more. The rocks above are at least a bit less than 1 billion years old. We have no better clue to the age of the rocks in the park than the exposures at Granite Park.

Despite the name, there is no granite at Granite Park, or anywhere else in or even near Glacier Park. Even though the diabase of the Purcell sill vaguely resembles granite in that both are speckled igneous rocks, the two rocks differ in most important respects. Most obviously, granite is very pale gray, diabase very dark gray, almost black in many places. Pieces of diabase from the Purcell sill are common nearly everywhere in the park. Watch the stream beds for pebbles of dark gray rock speckled with light crystals of feldspar about the size of rice grains.

Shepard & Kintla formations

The trail from the visitor center at Logan Pass to Hidden Lake is one of the best places to see the Shepard formation, about 1,000 feet of mostly red and tan mudstone. Nearly every outcrop along the higher part of that route is a natural museum of beautiful ripple marks and mudcracks, still exquisitely preserved almost a billion years after they formed. The upper part of the formation blends into about 1,000 feet of red mudstones that geologists call the Kintla formation. Most people look at the Kintla mudstones from a distance, because there is no place to see them at close range without a strenuous climb. Look at the red caps on many of the high mountains near the middle of the park.

The Shepard and Kintla formations are the youngest Precambrian rocks in the park. Even they contain no hint of the abundant animal life that would appear on earth a few hundred million years after they formed. In fact, the perfect preservation of very fine sedimentary details such as ripple marks and mudcracks in these rocks strongly suggests that animals had not yet appeared. In more recent times, digging and crawling animals have generally destroyed such structures long before the original soft sediments could harden into rock.

Above: *Single Shot Mountain shows the distinctive white-black-white banding of of Purcell diabase sill.*

Facing page: *Reynolds Mountain and Logan Pass.*

The Purcell diabase sill

The upper part of the Siyeh formation contains a conspicuous layer about 100 feet thick of black igneous rock called "diabase" sandwiched between layers of limestone. Molten magma squirted between sedimentary layers to form the layer of igneous rock. Geologists call an igneous intrusion formed that way a "sill." Precambrian sedimentary rocks throughout the northern Rocky Mountains contain hundreds of thick sills. This particularly conspicuous and well known example in Glacier Park is called the "Purcell sill."

R.C. GILDART

THE LEWIS OVERTHRUST

So far as anyone knows, the rocks we see in Glacier Park lay undisturbed until the Rocky Mountains formed sometime around 65 million years ago, give or take 10 million. All sorts of complex things happened as the Rocky Mountains formed, and the details need not concern us here because they do not greatly affect what we see in the park. One event that we do see clearly expressed in the landscape of Glacier Park was movement on the Lewis overthrust fault.

The large slab of Precambrian sedimentary rock that we see in the park slid eastward down a gently sloping surface that geologists call the "Lewis overthrust fault." No one knows exactly where the slab of Precambrian sedimentary rock came from, or exactly how far it moved. It must have come at least 35 miles, perhaps as far as 50 miles, conceivably farther. Neither does anyone know how long that movement lasted, but it was certainly not sudden, and probably continued for several million years at an imperceptibly slow pace. The fault appears in the landscape of the eastern part of the park.

At the Lewis overthrust fault, steep hills and cliffs of hard Precambrian rock rise abruptly above a softly rolling landscape eroded on much softer rocks beneath. The line of the fault exactly traces the eastern front of the mountains, where the rugged landscape of the Rocky Mountains meets the open expanse of the northern high plains. People driving beside St. Mary Lake cross the fault at the narrows near Rising Sun Campground, at a cliff of Altyn limestone.

Precambrian rocks above the Lewis overthrust fault lie on top of Cretaceous brown sandstones and black mudstones only about 100 million years old, the same rocks that lie beneath the high plains east of the park. The Cretaceous rocks below the Lewis overthrust fault accumulated in shallow sea water at the western margin of an island sea that then flooded much of central North America. Animal fossils do exist in the Cretaceous rocks, but they are hard to find because the Cretaceous rocks weather easily, and form very few good exposures.

The Lewis overthrust fault reverses the normal state of affairs in which the youngest rocks lie at the top of the stack, the oldest at the bottom. Glacier Park was one of the first places geologists found overthrust faults of this kind back in the 1890s, and it remains among the best places to see an overthrust fault. The best way to obtain a grand view of the Lewis overthrust fault is to look north from the top of Marias Pass on Highway 2 at the mountains in the southern edge of the park. You can see the tan Altyn limestone just above the fault as a straight band of tan rock that slopes like a railway grade descending down to the west.

We see the Lewis overthrust fault best expressed in Chief Mountain, a block of Precambrian sedimentary rock isolated by erosion from the rest of the overthrust slab. On all sides of Chief Mountain, the hard Precambrian sedimentary rocks rise in steep cliffs above the much softer Cretaceous sedimentary rocks that surround the mountain and continue beneath it.

North Fork Valley

We see another aspect of the Lewis overthrust fault in the North Fork Valley, which trends along the western margin of the park. It is about 10 miles wide, too broad to be an ordinary river valley. The width of that valley, and its remarkably straight north-to-south course, suggest that it must reflect bedrock structure. It seems reasonably clear that the North Fork Valley is a gap in the overthrust slab.

The Whitefish Range, west of the North Fork Valley, contains Precambrian sedimentary formations like those in Glacier Park. In Canada just north of Glacier, Cretaceous formations similar to those exposed in the high plains surface in the floor of the North Fork Valley. We would surely see the same formations in the western part of Glacier Park if the younger glacial sediments did not so completely cover the older rocks there.

The easiest way to explain the presence of Cretaceous rocks in the North Fork Valley is to assume that the overthrust slab broke into two. The fragment to become Glacier Park moved 10 miles farther east than the one that became the Whitefish Range. So the North Fork Valley is a window between the two parts of the overthrust slab. It looks down into the relatively young Cretaceous formations beneath ancient sedimentary rocks that we see in the mountains on either side. Compare the Precambrian rock that slid east on the Lewis overthrust fault to a slab of snow sliding down a roof, and then imagine the slab of snow separating into two large pieces exposing the roof between them.

Above: *Chief Mountain, the park's best example of the Lewis Overthrust.*

Facing page: *In the North Fork Valley, between the two pieces of Lewis Overthrust.*

15

Above and facing page: Grinnell Glacier.

ERODING THE MODERN LANDSCAPE

Movement on the Lewis overthrust fault created the major elements of the landscape; the blocks of mountains you might see from the moon, not the individual hills and valleys. Those are the legacy of at least 50 million years of patient erosional sculpture that still continues.

During most of the last 50 million or more years, the region had a desert climate, and erosion created landscapes much like those we see in the southwest desert today. Then, during the last 2 to 3 million years, a series of great ice ages brought enormous glaciers that carved most of the details of the modern landscape.

The desert years

During most of the past 50 million years, the entire region has had an extremely dry climate, perhaps similar to that of the modern southwest deserts. By the end of that time, streams had dissected the mountains of Glacier Park into a maze of deep and closely-spaced canyons, and deposited the debris of their erosion in a blanket of gravel spread far to the east. Although little, if anything, of the old desert landscape survives in the mountains, we can still see large remnants of the old high plains surface east of the mountains.

Erosion in dry regions tends to produce large expanses of smoothly graded plains underlain by layers of gravel laid down during occasional flash floods. Such plains did exist east of Glacier Park, east all the way to the Dakotas. The climate became wetter when the ice ages began, sometime between 2 and 3 million years ago, and modern streams have since carved their valleys into the old desert plains surface. Now, we see remnants of that old surface in the high uplands between streams. Look for their flat skyline profiles in the landscapes east of the mountain front.

The ice ages

Sometime between 2 and 3 million years ago the earth's climate changed, and great ice ages have come and gone ever since. No one knows what causes the great ice ages, or what ends them. Neither does anyone know how many ice ages there were, when they happened, or how long they lasted. Nor do we know when the next ice age will start, or what may herald its coming.

Those interesting and important questions need not concern us here. The glaciers that covered most of Glacier Park during the last ice age nearly obliterated the record of their predecessors, leaving a landscape that could as well have been created during a single ice age as during several. Almost everything we see in the modern landscape emerged in essentially its present form as the glaciers of the last ice age melted about 10,000 years ago.

During the height of the last ice age, glaciers as much as several thousand feet thick filled all the valleys in the park. Adjacent glaciers coalesced in many places to spread a nearly continuous ice cap over much of the high country. Many of the mountain glaciers in the western part of the park flowed into the North Fork Valley, ponding there to make a slowly-moving sheet of ice 10 miles across.

East of the park, glaciers pouring out of the mountains ponded on the high plains to make a broad expanse of nearly stagnant ice, a 'piedmont glacier' along the mountain front. Somewhere between Glacier Park and Browning, that piedmont glacier met and coalesced with the continental glacier spreading southwestward from central Canada. The seam is not obvious in the landscape, but we can determine just where the two glaciers joined by finding the line where glacially transported rocks from the Rocky Mountains meet the entirely different rocks carried in from northern Manitoba.

Glaciers

If more snow falls every winter than can melt the next summer, leftover snow accumulates from year to year and slowly turns into solid ice. As the ice reaches a depth of about 150 feet it begins to flow plastically as though it were extremely stiff modeling clay. When that happens, the patch of ice becomes a glacier. Some glaciers are hardly more than oversized snow patches, but those that carved the landscape of Glacier Park were real ice-age monsters, rivers of ice miles long and as much as several thousand feet deep in some places.

As far as anyone knows, glaciers that form on mountains never create new valleys. Instead, they invariably pour ponderously down stream valleys that already existed, changing them into glaciated stream valleys. Glaciers erode their valleys in some places, deposit the eroded sediments in others. The final result, after the ice melts, is a distinctive landscape that tells of glaciation in nearly every detail.

As a glacier moves down its valley, it descends into warmer climates, eventually reaching a level where the ice melts as fast as it advances. That balance stabilizes the front of the ice until the climate changes. An increase in the snowfall at high elevation will push the snout of the glacier to lower elevations, where the climate is warm enough to match the increased ice flow. Conversely, decreased snowfall at high elevations will reduce ice flow, causing the snout of the glacier to melt back to a higher, and cooler, elevation. As we might expect, glaciers respond to a warming climate by melting back to higher elevations, to a cooling climate by advancing to lower elevations.

The desert years

Glaciers carry enormous quantities of mud, sand and gravel embedded in the ice, especially in the lower part of the glacier. All that sediment makes the sole of the glacier rasp across bedrock surfaces as though it were a giant sheet of coarse sandpaper. After the glacier melts, the rasped bedrock surfaces are left smoothed, and covered with sets of parallel grooves called striations. Look almost anywhere in the park for such crudely sandpapered bedrock surfaces. The striations record the exact direction of ice movement. On a larger scale, the smoothed bedrock surfaces preserve a record of where the ice flowed, and where other processes of erosion shaped the bedrock. That record still survives in some areas of Glacier Park 10,000 years after the great glaciers melted.

Look high up the cliffs almost anywhere in the park to see that their lower parts are relatively smooth, their highest parts extremely rough. The smooth lower parts and rougher upper parts meet along a sharp line that slopes gently down the valley. That line marks the ice level on the cliff during the height of the last ice age. Sediment embedded in the glacier rasped the lower part of the cliff smooth, while freezing and thawing pried blocks out of the rock above the ice, leaving that part of the cliff ragged. The old ice level is especially easy to see on the cliffs high above Logan Pass and Two Medicine Lake.

In areas where the old ice level is well preserved, it is possible to trace it with the eye from one mountain side to another to reconstruct mentally the glaciers that existed during the last ice age. By doing that, we can see that ice completely filled many a valley and spilled over a divide to coalesce with a glacier in the next valley. Many large areas of the park must have lain beneath an almost continuous ice cap. In much of Glacier Park only the higher peaks rose above the expanse of ice.

Giant quarrying machine

Glaciers erode bedrock mostly by freezing fast to blocks of rock already broken along ancient fractures, and then pulling them loose, a process called "plucking." Glacially-plucked bedrock surfaces look ragged, as though crudely quarried. Look at almost any of the high cliffs in the park to see examples of glacially plucked surfaces.

The heads of glaciers pluck chunks of bedrock loose more efficiently than any other part. As it moves down-slope, the ice draws away from the bedrock behind it, pulling blocks of bedrock loose and opening a gap between rock and ice. Anyone who walks to the head of a glacier must cross that gap to get back onto bedrock, and in many cases that requires quite a jump. Snow and meltwater fill that gap with new ice that freezes fast to the bedrock. Meanwhile, the glacier continues to move down its valley and repeats the process, pulling more chunks of rock loose, and opening again the gap between ice and bedrock. Now that the ice has melted, we can see how deeply the heads of the ice age glaciers quarried the mountaintops.

Every glacial valley heads in a large hollow called a "cirque," perhaps the most characteristic element of glaciated mountain landscapes. There are hundreds of cirques in Glacier Park. Nearly every peak drops away into cirques on at least one side, most on several sides. In many places, adjacent cirques blend into each other, making it hard to see them individually. In other places, cirques stand alone, looking as though a giant had gouged the mountain with an oversized ice cream scoop. Sparkling little lakes nestle in the floors of many cirques, reflecting the cliffs of the headwall rising to the peak above. Hidden Lake, Avalanche Lake, and Iceberg Lake all are good examples of cirque lakes familiar to many park visitors.

Where several glaciers flowed down a mountain, gouging cirques into the summit from several directions, we now see the jagged remnant of the original peak. It forms a ragged pinnacle that drops away in steep cliffs into the deep cirques below. We call those rocky spires "horn" peaks, an alpine term familiar in the names of such famous mountains as the Matterhorn. Most of the high peaks in Glacier Park are horns.

Gouged valleys

Every summer, people expose thousands of dollars of film recording views of distant peaks reflected in the waters of Lake McDonald or St. Mary Lake. Those really are remarkable scenes, and they could not exist if the great ice age glaciers had not gouged the valleys straight so we could look along them at the mountains in the distance.

Glaciers are less flexible than rivers, and cannot flow so easily around bends in the valleys. So, they removed the bends from the original river valley as though they were bulldozers going down a narrow mountain trail. That also leaves the valley considerably wider

BRECK P. KENT

Above: *Hikers on Grinnell Glacier are dwarfed by the Garden Wall.*
Left: *Grinnell Glacier.*

Facing page: *Sunset over Lake McDonald.*

19

than it was before glaciation. And it changes the cross-sectional profile.

Large glaciers tend to gouge their valleys into deeply rounded troughs almost semi-circular in cross-section. We see that best in the higher parts of glaciated valleys where very little sediment fills the floor. The bedrock floors of those high parts of the glaciated valley typically contain small lakes or ponds called "tarns." You can tell that tarns fill a bedrock basin by going to the outlet stream and watching it spill over solid rock.

Glaciers gnaw the ridges separating adjacent valleys into thin rock walls with ragged crests generally called "aretes," a term imported from the Swiss Alps where the glaciated landscapes resemble those in Glacier Park. The Garden Wall is a good example of an arete familiar to many park visitors. It is so thin near its crest that in one place there is a hole in it. In the Many Glacier area, people enjoy watching the sun shine for a moment through that window as it sets behind the Garden Wall. Before glaciation, that thin wall of rock was the crest of a broad ridge.

Where active glaciers met, their surfaces join at the same level. Now that the ice has melted and exposed the floors of those glaciated valleys, we can see that small glaciers do not carve as deeply as do large glaciers. Tributary valleys stand well above the main valley, and their streams join the main stream over waterfalls or cascades. An example of this is Birdwoman Falls, seen by most park visitors as they drive along the valley of McDonald Creek

Glacial moraines

Melting glacial ice dumps a deposit of indiscriminately mixed mud, sand, gravel and boulders. That material, which looks in a roadcut like something a bulldozer might have scraped together, is called "till." It is easy to recognize even where there is no roadcut because glaciers leave boulders littering the surfaces of most deposits. Geologists call any deposit of till a "moraine."

There are several kinds of moraines that differ in origin according to the part of the glacier that deposited them, and also differ in appearance. Let's start with the most distinctive kind.

Glaciers deposit a ridge of till around their lower margins where a balance between the rates of ice advance and melting puts an end to the glacial conveyor belt. The result is a "terminal moraine" that faithfully records the outline of the lower part of the glacier that built it. We don]t see very many good examples of terminal moraines within Glacier Park, because so many of the valley glaciers emptied into either the big piedmont ice sheet along the eastern margin of the park, or the huge glacier that filled the North Fork Valley. However, there are a few small moraines at high elevations that appear to have formed since the last ice age ended.

Glaciers also deposit till along their margins to build "lateral moraines," which make high benches along the vlaley walls. Lateral moraines are especially prominent on south-facing valley walls at low elevations because more ice melts in those places, and therefore deposits more sediment. Large lateral moraines exist along the lower parts of most of the valleys in the park, and in some places they become very prominent indeed. The ridges on both sides of Lake McDonald, for example, are large laterial moraines, perhaps the

DOUG DYE

STEVE KAUFMAN

Above: *Sperry Glacier.*
Left: *Sedimentary rock strata of Haystack Butte.*

Facing page: *A lateral morain on Heavens Peak.*

21

JEFF GNASS

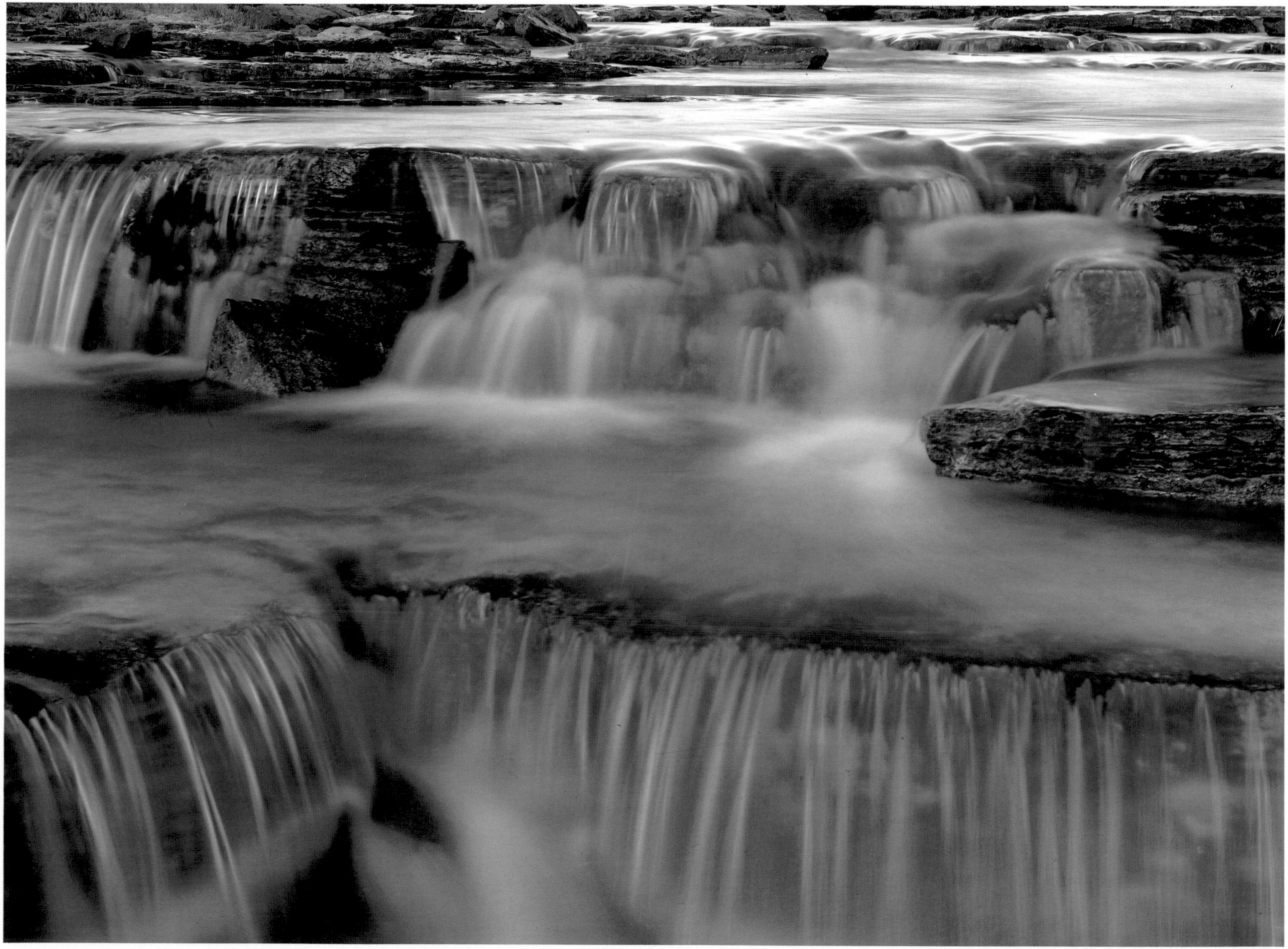

most spectacular in the park. And the densely wooded hills along the south side of St. Mary Lake are other large lateral moraines.

Finally, melting glaciers plaster much of the ground beneath them with till to create a rather characterless deposit called a "ground moraine." Most of the large valleys in the park have ground moraine here and there in their floors, but we rarely notice them except as expanses of gently undulating valley floor full of small ponds and marshes. Glacial till is generally fairly impermeable to water, and ground moraine is especially so because it was compacted beneath the weight of the glacier.

Glacial outwash

We think of ice ages as cold times, and the climate probably was significantly colder and much wetter than what we know today. However, there is no reason to doubt that ice age summers were warm, quite possibly as warm as the summers we know. The summer days were long then, too, and many must have been sunny. We are, after all, descended from people who camped out during the last ice age, and our ancestors seem to have managed quite well.

We know, because we can see the results, that vast quantities of ice melted off the lower parts of the ice age glaciers every summer, shedding torrents of muddy water into the streams. The swollen and muddy streams dropped part of their sediment load to form deposits that geologists call "outwash." We can look at the streams that drain from glaciers in Alaska and Canada today, and imagine what ours must have been like then: many small and constantly shifting channels picking their way through a maze of islands. But the muddiest season came as the glaciers melted at the end of the ice age.

Everything we see suggests that the last ice age ended abruptly. At the height of the last ice age, about 11,000 or 12,000 years ago, so much water was tied up in the great glaciers that sea level stood some 300 feet lower than it now does. Then the climate changed and, within 2,500 years, sea level had risen to its present stand, which means that the land ice had melted back to about what we see today. Even though we don't know how or why the climate changed, we can easily image what the land to be Glacier Park was like during those 2,500 years.

The place was, quite simply, a mess.

Rapidly melting glaciers shed torrents of incredibly muddy water, and leave behind them dreary expanses of watery mud and gravel. In Glacier Park, all that debris still lies just as the melting glaciers left it about 10,000 years ago. Nothing has changed except that trees have grown since then, and they make things look nicer. Consider Lake McDonald and St. Mary Lake, both relics of the last years of the last ice age.

Lake McDonald formed as the glaciers melted. Evidently, a large mass of ice was left behind as the glacier rapidly melted back, and muddy meltwater washed sediment in around it, perhaps partially burying it. When that marooned expanse of ice finally melted some hundreds or perhaps thousands of

Right: *Beargrass near Sperry Glacier, with Grinnell mudstone in foreground.*
Facing page: *The cascades of the Hanging Gardens.*

Right: *The rocky shore of Lake McDonald.*

Facing page: *Grinnell mudstone and a high mountain stream just below Sperry Glacier.*

years later, it left the basin that the lake now fills. St. Mary Lake formed at the same time, although in a different way. Glacial meltwater washing into the valley from tributary canyons on both sides deposited large fans of gravel that now impound the lake. The park entrance and visitor center at the lower end of St. Mary Lake stand on that deposit of gravel. Similar situations exist in the lower parts of most of the large valleys in the park.

AFTER THE ICE AGE

Now that the great ice age glaciers are gone, at least for the time being, other processes of erosion are slowly changing the mountains of Glacier Park. Nevertheless, most of what we see is still left from the last ice age, not the product of modern processes of erosion.

Now streams of water flow along the floors of valleys filled to the brim with ice a little more than 10,000 years ago. The water is slowly shaping the floors of those valleys into the forms that streams create, but they have not made much progress. The waterfalls and cascades are all remnants of glacial erosion, and will all disappear as the streams continue their own work.

The big lakes trap most of the sediment that the modern streams carry and every particle of mud or grain of sand brings the lake closer to its end. Before too many thousands of years have passed, all the lakes will have filled with sediment, and become level plains. In the geologic sense of time, all lakes are temporary, and doomed to quick disappearance.

Meanwhile, the tediously slow processes of weather are beginning to break the bare rock into soil, and thus to soften the harsh outlines of the glaciated mountains. However, that is an extremely slow process, and one cannot help wondering how far it may progress before another ice age intervenes. To see how slowly weathering proceeds, look at the glacially striated bedrock surfaces almost anywhere in the park, and remember that they have probably been ice free and exposed to the elements for approximately 10,000 years. It is impossible to ponder the freshness of those surfaces without reflecting that soil is not a renewable resource within any humanly meaningful time span, and that soil erosion really does impose an irreparable loss.

Finally, the modern glaciers: Compared to their predecessors of the last ice age, they are nothing. And they have diminished greatly in both size and number since they were first mapped just after the turn of the 20th century. Such small—perhaps minuscule is the better word—glaciers could not by any stretch of the imagination carve the magnificent landscape we see in Glacier Park. Furthermore, the little glaciers we see in the park today appear to be new glaciers that formed sometime after the last ice age, not the shrunken remnants of the ice age giants. The modern glaciers have carved small cirques around the edges of some of the big cirques left from the last ice age, and they have made a few moraines high in the mountains. Otherwise, they have contributed very little to the landscape of Glacier Park.

But who knows? Someday those little glaciers we see in the highest and shadiest valleys of Glacier Park may grow into the next generation of giants when the next ice age begins.

Peopling the Park

Facing page: The autumn mood of Lake McDonald.

by C.W. Buchholtz

Glacier's rocky peaks, deep-blue lakes and dense forests have long put out a call to people. Primitive pathways must have lured Native American hunters. And we know its cliffs and echoes made enough magic to stimulate legends. The fur trade brought a handful of trappers and traders cautiously venturing through. Mountain passes caught the eyes of railroad engineers and likely-looking rocks kept prospectors prowling. Vacant land drew pioneers. Scenic land brought tourists. The abuse of land made conservationists decide to protect this region, and simple aesthetics made others wish to preserve it for future generations. Solitude and natural beauty attracted people looking for rest and recreation.

The wilderness itself reminds us of the past, the way things used to look. It offers a stark contrast to everyday scenes crowded with cars and concrete. It makes us wonder about all those earlier travelers who heard the mountains' call. Even an outline of their visits may help us appreciate what little wild country remains, still preserved for our pleasure.

TRIBES AND TRAILS

Exactly who first traveled the trails of today's Glacier Park remains a mystery, despite extensive archaeological exploration here in recent years. Some day, archaeologists may find an ancient campsite, a cache of tools or some other clues to provide us with a clearer prehistoric picture. Meanwhile, we can only speculate about ancient hunters who haunted these mountains. Chances are good that prehistoric hunters roamed through this region thousands of years ago, but evidence of their activity is scant. A few circles of rocks marking old tipi rings still may be spotted along the eastern foothills. An old buffalo skull once was found atop Chief Mountain. But stones and bones merely hint at Indian pursuits of religious beliefs.

Our first documented glimpse of the region was provided by Hudson's Bay Company agent Peter Fidler. He was traveling with a Piegan band of Blackfeet Indians, southwestward across the Canadian prairies in 1792. A map Fidler later produced displayed a rough sketch of the Rockies and the name of "Kings Mountain" attached to one of those peaks. Later changed to "Chief Mountain," that prominent landmark of the front range became the first of Glacier's features to gain recognition. What Peter Fidler also discovered, as did a few other traders who probed this area, was the fact that powerful bands of Blackfeet (Blackfoot in Canada) Indians dominated the entire upper Missouri River region and the headwaters of the Saskatchewan River as well.

At that time the Blackfeet Confederation consisted of the Siksika (Northern Blackfeet), the Kainah (Bloods), and the Piegan (Pikuni). Allied with them were the Gros Ventre (or Big Belly). These warlike bands had extended their power throughout the plains during the 1700s, just after they obtained horses and guns. Their reputation as fearsome warriors spread quickly. Their dominion included vast herds of bison, now theirs to hunt. With plentiful food, and hides for clothing, shelter and equipment, the Blackfeet clearly were masters of Montana's northern plains by the 1790s. For them, Glacier's Rockies acted as a massive western boundary. And upon occasion, small raiding parties of aggressive Blackfeet ventured across the mountains to prey upon tribes of the western slope. Glacier's high passes served those war parties well. Very rarely did the Blackfeet bother to hunt mountain animals, however, since their horses and life-style were geared to the prairie.

More accustomed to the mountains were several Indian tribes far less powerful than the Blackfeet. The Kutenai, the Kalispel (or Pend d'Oreille) and the Flathead tribes ranged throughout the forested valleys of western Montana. Until the Blackfeet forced them off the plains, these tribes also had lived and hunted on the prairie. In making the mountains their home, they adopted deer and elk, fish and fowl, berries and camas roots as their staples—substitutes for the favored buffalo. Once or twice a year, hunting parties from these western tribes bravely ventured east across the mountains, entering the plains to hunt buffalo at the risk of a Blackfeet attack. One rare tale of such a clash placed the event near Glacier's Cut Bank Creek. There Siyeh (Mad Wolf) and his band of Blackfeet warriors fought some Kutenai who were attempting to return westward across Cut Bank Pass. The Blackfeet, according to the tale, slaughtered and scalped all the Kutenai except for one old woman.

Violence and hostility kept the western tribes confined to the mountains. But their lifestyles adjusted quickly. The Kutenai, in particular, developed a reputation for being skilled hunters of mountain sheep. Observers marveled at their ability to run up steep slopes and early explorers noted that their leg muscles developed an abnormal size from climbing across ridges.

Another minor band of Indians also frequented the region. Called the Mountain Assiniboine (or Stonies), this group subsisted along the eastern

Blackfeet Indians at Cracker Lake.

epidemics, and whiskey reduced their numbers and will to fight did the Blackfeet weaken their grip upon this land. Gradually trappers and trading posts became more common. Disappearing buffalo herds spelled the end of the prosperity of food and materials, and starvation was common among the Blackfeet by the 1880s. At the same time, prospectors were demanding that the Blackfeet relinquish their mountain land. In 1895, the Blackfeet sold the "Ceded Strip" (Glacier's eastern side) for $1.5 million. Decades earlier, western-slope tribes had relinquished all claims to these mountains. Still, today's Blackfeet Reservation, adjacent to Glacier's eastern boundary, reminds us of earlier Native American stewardship over the entire region.

TRAPPERS AND TRAVELERS

Indian hostility kept most mountain men away from Glacier. Only a handful of trappers or traders left any account of their journeys across these mountains. In 1810, to give one rare example, trapper Finian MacDonald and 150 Indian allies crossed through Marias Pass headed toward the plains. Almost immediately they encountered 170 "Peeagans." The ensuing battle left seven Blackfeet dead and taught men like MacDonald to choose safer routes far to the north or south. Other fur traders simply skirted the region. And only sketchy evidence links the search for beaver pelts with Glacier's waterways. Both Lake McDonald and tiny Rubideau Creek may derive their names from such adventurers.

Missionaries and map makers also traveled through quickly. Exactly which "Black Robe" paused to christen St. Mary Lake remains a question, but maps soon would display that appellation. In the early 1850s "official" explorers began arriving. Engineer A.W. Tinkham, associated with the Isaac I. Stevens survey, traveled across Glacier in 1853 as he searched for potential railroad routes. He crossed Cut Bank Pass and noted that any railroad built there would require a huge tunnel. In the following year, Stevens dispatched John Doty, who more carefully surveyed all of Glacier's eastern slope. But Doty concluded that none of the mountain passes he observed was suitable for a railroad, leaving Marias Pass to be "rediscovered" in 1889 by another engineer, John F. Stevens.

Other government surveyors arrived by 1860, this time marking the 49th parallel as the international boundary. With them came artist James Madison Alden, who produced the first scenic watercolors of Glacier's northern mountains. By the 1860s and 1870s a few prospectors wandered along the western slope. In one sketchy (albeit surprising) report, a 30-ounce nugget of gold supposedly was found at Quartz Lake. Those decades also introduced a few itinerant whiskey traders, distributing their products among the Indians along the eastern slope. One such "whiskey fort" established by John Kennedy is remembered only by the name of today's Kennedy Creek.

Additional government surveys in 1874 brought Lt. John Van Orsdale, dispatched to observe this area from Fort Shaw. After visiting Lake McDonald

foothills. Forced by the Blackfeet to accept less desirable hunting grounds, the Stonies gained their name from their method of cooking food with heated rocks. The Stonies were few in number and always fearful of their more aggressive neighbors. Deer and elk served as their food supply, with lesser animals like porcupine adding to their diet when hunting was bad. They chewed tree bark if starvation was imminent.

Years of hunting and warfare sparked numerous legends and tales. Writers like George Bird Grinnell in the 1880s and James Willard Schultz in the 1920s recorded many Indian stories, some associated with Glacier's mountains. Grinnell's stories of Napi (or Old Man) and the Blackfeet Genesis are particularly poignant. In part because of Grinnell's and Schultz's writings, a pantheon of Indian chiefs' and heroes' names became attached to Glacier's landscape. Dotting the map are sites named Red Eagle, Curly Bear, Heavy Runner and Mad Wolf, all recalling famous Indian leaders. Medicine Grizzly, Beaver Medicine and Windmaker evoke the stuff of legends. A few Indian names predated Grinnell and Schultz, with Two Medicine Valley obtaining its name from two ceremonial lodges that once graced the area. St. Mary Lakes were called The Lakes Inside before white man arrived.

Through much of the 19th century, Blackfeet power kept visitors or invaders away from this territory. Not until constant war, recurrent smallpox

(which he called Lake Terry after his commanding officer), traveling up Nyack Creek, and crossing Cut Bank Pass, Van Orsdale was sufficiently impressed by the country to write a letter suggesting that the region be made a national park. With Yellowstone Park founded only two years earlier, Van Orsdale believed he had spotted another national treasure. But more than two decades would pass before others found merit in his suggestion.

The 1880s ushered in the man who would ensure that the national park idea would succeed. As an authority on Indians and as editor of *Forest and Stream* magazine, George Bird Grinnell was influential as well as politically knowledgeable. He originally came to the region to publicize the starving and destitute condition of the Blackfeet. But big-game hunting drew him toward the mountains, and he returned to explore for many years. He also wrote of his experiences in 14 essays for *Forest and Stream*. Grinnell concluded that "The scenery is grand, game plenty, the fishing unexcelled," and offered the nation the first real publicity about Glacier's mountains. Soon other men of wealth journeyed here to hunt, with the Baring family of English bankers, Ralph Pulitzer and Henry L. Stimson typifying adventurers of that era. Geographical names in Glacier including Singleshot, Fusillade, Gunsight, and Baring are a few mementos left by those hunters.

Prospectors also explored this region, with "Dutch Lui" Myers being

Above: *Two Guns White Calf, one of the models for the Indian portrayed on the buffalo nickel, was a Montana Blackfeet leader.*
Center: *James Willard Shultz (at right in picture) lived among the Blackfeet as a young man before the tribe was reservation-bound.*
Left: *Heavy Runner Mountain, named for a Blackfeet leader.*

29

among the first to find a vein of what he described as "grayish white quartz carrying gold, silver, copper, and some lead" in 1889. But getting the mountains opened to legal prospecting took another nine years. Meanwhile, James J. Hill's Great Northern Railway was snaking its way westward. Once surveyor John F. Stevens declared Marias Pass usable, construction proceeded up Summit Creek and across the Continental Divide, then descended along Bear Creek eventually to parallel the Middle Fork of the Flathead River. Almost overnight, civilization sprouted along the route of the Great Northern Railway, which began service in 1891. Travelers came in greater numbers, with a few taking the time to wander toward spots like Lake McDonald. One of those tourists was Dr. Lyman Sperry. A college professor and traveling lecturer, Dr. Sperry was on the lookout for scenic attractions, hoping to add subjects to his lecture list and helping the Great Northern publicize their new route. What enchanted Sperry most was alpine scenery. His interest in glaciers led him to declare that "a man can find anything he wants in this region."

CRUSADERS OF COMMERCE AND CONSERVATION

The coming of the railroad introduced a handful of settlers to the western valleys. People like Milo Apgar, Charlie Howe, George Snyder and a few others carved some homesteads out of the forested shoreline of Lake McDonald. Other hardy pioneers drifted to likely spots farther north, especially where meadowlands offered natural fields. Valleys adjacent to the North Fork of the Flathead River soon boasted a few ranches. The settlers around Lake McDonald quickly realized that scenery was one of their most profitable resources. They began to cater to railway travelers, providing meals and cabins and boat rides up the lake. A few acted as guides. An infant "Glacier Hotel" soon appeared at the upper end of the lake near Snyder Creek, later to be expanded and become Lake McDonald Lodge. The tourist business had begun.

Back-country trails, however, served more than just tourists. Persistent prospectors kept searching for signs of wealth. Some promising veins offered hints of copper. Mineral Creek, far up the McDonald Valley, became the site of early exploration and investment by people like Elizabeth Collins, the "Cattle Queen of Montana." With the eastern slope opened to prospecting in 1898, a flood of excitement and expectation overwhelmed the region. Dozens of claims were filed, many people believing that their strikes would prove as rich as Butte. The settlement of Saint Mary was born in this boom. To the north, in today's Many Glacier area, the town of Altyn claimed its leadership of the Swiftcurrent mining district. Several hundred prospectors pawed at nearby slopes. Exploration shafts were sunk, companies were formed, investment was attracted, a few mines were developed. But yields proved dismal. The boom went bust. Within a year or two most of the miners had left, although a few diehards held on for another decade or more.

At the same time, however, the discovery of oil to the north in Alberta—

Left: *Packing a horse at Haunted Lake, about 1907, with Porcupine Ridge in background.*
Far left: *Frank Liebig, one of a handful of robust early-day forest rangers who worked to protect Glacier country before it became a park.*

Facing page: *Blackfeet Indians at Trick Falls, about 1917.*

and also near Kintla Lake—spurred a bit more excitement. A primitive road was carved from Lake McDonald through the forests to the Kintla region, with exploration rigs soon to follow. Small deposits of gas and oil also were discovered in the valleys of the eastern slope. But like the dreams of copper and gold, oil proved to be insufficient to sustain investment. Interest in mining and drilling waned and by 1907 it was clear that mineral wealth could not be found.

In addition to railroaders, homesteaders and prospectors, some people with a less exploitive outlook also discovered these mountains. Along with writers and publicists like Grinnell and Sperry came others intending to protect the region. As part of a national conservation movement, Congress permitted the establishment of forest reserves (later called national forests) in 1891. That same year the Lewis and Clark Forest Reserve was established, which included Glacier's western slope. (Glacier's eastern slope would be added after 1898.) In terms of actual protection or regulation, little changed until 1900. By then, forest rangers had started patrolling the region. Frank Herrig and Frank Liebig guarded against abuses and waste. They fought forest fires, enforced game laws, watched for timber thieves, looked after tourists, and kept the trails open. It was their intent to provide for the orderly development and use of the region's resources.

At the same time, a few people believed that mere conservation did not provide enough protection for the scenic treasures of this region. Advocates of the national park idea began gaining influence, especially once the search for minerals proved futile. George Bird Grinnell, one of the most influential spokesmen for the park idea, promoted the cause in a 1901 article for *Century Magazine* entitled "The Crown of the Continent." He argued that recreational and aesthetic concerns demanded more attention in the form of protection. Men like Grinnell and Sperry helped convince Great Northern Railway officials to support the national park concept for Glacier, a politically important move.

On December 11, 1907, Montana's Senator Thomas H. Carter introduced a bill to create Glacier National Park. Several years of public debate followed. A few local homesteaders feared the loss of their land. Critics of the Great Northern argued that a park would preclude using any of the mountain passes for a competitive railroad route. Some people believed that timber and other park resources—especially wildlife—should be harvested rather than preserved. Nevertheless, those voices of opposition never shouted in unison. And proponents of the park made a few compromises regarding rights of private land owners, valid mineral claims and water development projects. Compared with other conservation fights, the move to establish Glacier Park was not very controversial. On May 11, 1910, President William Howard Taft signed the bill creating Glacier National Park.

BUILDERS OF A NATIONAL PLAYGROUND

Glacier's first superintendent, Major William R. Logan, arrived in August of 1910. He faced a virtual wilderness (just then plagued by a dry summer during which forest fires blackened nearly 50,000 acres within the park). Logan began his work that season by appointing a ranger force of six men. He also surveyed the region, formulating ideas about developing Glacier into a "playground" more acceptable to modern tourists. Working with other national park planners, Logan later proposed building an extensive grid of roadways, a plethora of hotels, and a vast network of trails. Of all his ideas, the "Transmountain Road" concept proved most popular, later to become Going-to-the-Sun Road.

But plans of Superintendent Logan and his successors paled in comparison to the immediate investment and construction initiated by the Great Northern Railway. Between 1910 and 1917, the Great Northern spent $1.5 million developing tourist facilities in Glacier. Nine rustic chalets were constructed at various back-country locations (with today's Granite Park and Sperry chalets still remaining); three tent camps offered more primitive shelters; and a "Mammoth Mountain" hotel was built at Many Glacier, costing a half million dollars. Belton Chalet (at West Glacier) and Glacier Park Lodge (at Midvale, now East Glacier) rested just outside the park near the railroad's depots. A network of roads and trails was built to link these various accommodations.

Over the next two decades, people who visited Glacier followed patterns established by the Great Northern and its hotel company. A majority of tourists arrived by train, disembarking near the large hotel at East Glacier. Riding horses through the park became the primary mode of travel. From East Glacier, trail riders rode to Two Medicine Chalet. From there they headed to Cut Bank Chalet and on to Saint Mary Chalet and Going-to-the-Sun Chalet, crossing the Continental Divide and reboarding the train at West Glacier. Lake launches and auto-bus trips offered optional means of approaching scenic areas. The railroad literature encouraged people to hike as well. At least a week was required to see the park in the manner prescribed for the typical tourist, with some people taking a month or more to "do" Glacier.

That genteel style of tourism became outdated with the building of the Transmountain Road. Once the National Park Service was established, in 1916, funds for such major development projects became available. Surveys conducted in 1917 and 1918 settled the new route across the Continental Divide through Logan Pass. Actual construction took more than a decade and the cost was some $3 million. On July 15, 1933, Going-to-the-Sun Road officially opened. It was a highway intended for "the great mass of people" cutting through the heart of the park, and meant to introduce visitors to Glacier's wilderness.

Whether that roadway beckoned people into the back country could be questioned. Going-to-the-Sun Road certainly altered the way tourists explored the park. Instead of spending a week or a month winding and

Above: Rising Wolf Camp, 1917
Left: Stephen Mather, first Superintendent of National Parks, who conceived the idea of an over-the-divide road in the park.

Facing page: Lunch Creek and Mount Reynolds, with Going-to-the-Sun Road.

33

The automobile age reaches Glacier National Park:
Right: Two Medicine Chalet.
Far right: On the road to the summit in July.
Below left: Early-day travel had its hazards.
Below right: Glacier Park Hotel.

34

wandering along back-country trails, they could view the "heart" of Glacier in a day. Instead of depending upon chalets or tipi camps for food and shelter, they favored campgrounds and motels. In the years to come, an estimated 95 percent of Glacier's visitors confined their visits to that narrow ribbon of roadway. Statistics proved that building the road was a popular idea: only 40,000 people toured the park in 1925, but 210,000 people traveled through in 1936. With this influx of people and automobiles, more facilities were added to provide for the new style of vacationing, with campgrounds and picnic areas (and visitor centers by the 1960s) making the scenic roadway more like a corridor of civilization. Meanwhile, the old and disused chalets and tent camps were destroyed or removed. The tempo of a Glacier Park visit grew faster, accommodations were designed for more people and shorter stays. By the late 1960s, one estimate showed the average visitor remained in the Glacier area for 25 hours.

But during the 1960s a preservationist philosophy began to challenge the value of roadways and rapid visits. An awakened interest in and concern for the environment led more people to forsake their cars to investigate Glacier's back country. More hikers meant more sophisticated management techniques, and restrictions were imposed to preserve wilderness values. Adding to that mood, the Wilderness Act of 1964 mandated that vast natural areas within Glacier and other national parks be protected from any further encroachments by civilization.

People demanding environmental quality asked probing questions about the preservation of Glacier's unique features. Concern over the purity of the park's air meant monitoring neighboring industries. Realizing the park's water could be polluted led to refurbishing sanitary facilities. Studies of eagles and elk, grizzlies and ground squirrels, natural fire and a host of other ecological concerns helped highlight that Glacier, in 1974, was unique enough to be named one of the World Biosphere Reserves. People slowly rediscovered the fact that Glacier Park was more than just a rapidly passing scene on a cross-country tour. It was a place to be pondered; a place to be preserved and enjoyed.

The call of the mountains changed through the years. The roar of the wind and waterfalls, the whisper of pines and the echoing call of loons gradually mixed with the hoofbeats of Indian ponies and the muffled tread of Indian trackers. The voices of trappers and traders, explorers and exploiters soon mingled with the curses of miners and the laughter of tourists. The mountains called with an almost mystical allure. At times these Rockies offered passage to the plains; beckoned with the temptation of wealth; and stirred the spirit of adventure. In Glacier National Park, the call of the mountains still can be heard.

Triple arches supporting Going-to-the-Sun Road.

KATHY AHLENSLAGER

© HILEMAN

3003   GOING-TO-THE-SUN CHALETS, GLACIER NATIONAL PARK   5A-H214

PHOTO BY HILEMAN

8145   SPERRY GLACIER, GLACIER NATIONAL PARK   5A-H2

A Merry Christmas and Happy New Year

TWO MEDICINE LAKE

214   GREETINGS FROM MONTANA ~

PHOTO BY HILEMAN

8136   GOING-TO-THE-SUN HIGHWAY, GLACIER NATIONAL PARK   5A-H22

KAREN KNIE-THOMPSON

KATHY AHLENSLAGER

HINKE/SACILOTTO

BRUCE HANDS

Top left: *View of the Garden Wall from Logan Pass Visitor Center, with International Peace Park symbols.*

Top right: *The United States-Canada border.*

Bottom left: *The classic Glacier National Park tour bus.*

Bottom right: *Interior of Glacier Park Lodge made with logs 36 to 42 inches in diameter and 40 feet long.*

Facing page: *Postcards celebrating the West's newest playground.*

37

THE ASCENT OF CHIEF MOUNTAIN

by R.C. "Bert" Gildart

In the northeastern corner of Glacier National Park, country that was once the domain of the Blackfeet Indian, stands a turret-shaped mountain. This geological oddity, on the plains east of the main range, has attracted the attention of explorers and mapmakers from the earliest times. Its existence was first noted on the Arrowsmith maps, published in England in 1796, upon which it is called "Kings Mountain." Peter Fidler, who supplied the information for these maps, visited this area in 1792, and was the first white man to record this landmark.

Meriwether Lewis also saw the mountain from a vantage far to the south, and he called it Tower Mountain. Once the mountain was referred to as "Kaiser Peak," but none of those names ever stuck. Appropriately, the name is derived from the Blackfeet Indians who have always held it in awe, as "Old Chief," "Mountain-of-the-Chief," or simply, "Chief Mountain."

Legend has it that in the early days only one Blackfeet ever attempted to climb the mountain. The attempt was made more than 150 years ago. A hunting party of young men were encamped at its base, and one of the youngest and most ambitious of the young warriors declared that he would go to the summit. His companions watched him from below until he passed out of sight along one of the very highest ledges. Then the Spirit of the mountain must have met him, for although the rest of the band waited many days, the young warrior never returned. Thereafter, the Blackfeet avoided any close acquaintance with the Chief.

Perhaps the warrior's wish to climb the mountain was based on his recollection of a Flathead legend the Blackfeet treasured and added to their own.

The story concerns a Flathead warrior, a man watched over by a spirit so mighty that no peril of battle or of the hunt could overcome him. When at last in his old age he came to die, he told the young men his long kept secret. Many years before, as the time approached for him to go alone into the forest and seek the vision that would be his guide and protection throughout life, he sought a spot and a spirit that never before had been tried. Carrying the usual sacred bison skull for his pillow, he had crossed the mountains and journeyed east into the far-off Blackfeet country. Then, with none to aid him save the steady power of his own courage, he ventured upon the ledges of the "Chief-of-All-Mountain." There, choking down each gasp of panic when wind and overhanging walls tested his endurance, the warrior finally forced his way up to the very top. For four days and nights he paced the summit, chanting warrior songs, attempting to make peace with the gods who were to decide his destiny.

It is said the Spirit of the mountain attempted to drive him off the peak during his vigil. On each of the first three nights, with ever increasing violence, the Spirit had come to him and threatened to hurl him off the face of the cliff if he did not go down on the following day. But each time he refused. Instead he spent each day pacing the summit, chanting his warrior song and waving his peace pipe in the air. Finally, on the fourth night, the Spirit yielded, giving him the token of his life. In later years none of the young Flatheads ever dared to follow their great warrior's example, and for almost half a century he remained the only man who had braved the Spirit of the Chief and made it his friend.

The legend might have a basis in fact. In 1891, Henry Stimson, Secretary of State during the Hoover administration and Secretary of War during the Franklin Roosevelt administration, journeyed to the Chief Mountain area and felt the challenge of the mountain. Three friends, including a full-blooded Blackfeet Indian, began their ascent on a blustery summer day. His journals recall the climb—and their findings!

"Two hundred feet up," wrote Stimson, "came our first trouble, perhaps the worst of the day. We were sidling along a narrow shelf, with arms outstretched against the wall above, when we reached a spot where the shelf was broken by a round protruding shoulder. Beyond it, the ledge commenced again and it seemed to offer our only way upward. I was leading at the time and, after examining it, turned back to a wider portion of the shelf for consolation. It was not a place one would care to try if there was an alternative."

The journal continues, noting the frustration of the party and difficulty they had negotiating the shale rock. Still they plodded on, and Stimson's journal records their progress as they neared the summit.

"Six or seven hundred feet more of steady work, and we could feel the summit breeze beginning to blow down the narrow chimney." "Billy," their Blackfeet guide, was then sent to the front, and at half past one, the first Blackfeet Indian stepped out on the summit of Chief Mountain.

"The summit," wrote Stimson, "is a long ridge of disintegrated rock flanked at either end by lower rounded turrets, and at its highest part is no wider than a New England stone wall. On the opposite western side the cliffs fell away as on our own, but they seemed shorter, were composed of looser rock, and far down below we could see steep slopes of shale meeting them part way. After we had picked out our various landmarks in the wonderful outlook about us, and I had made my record from compass and barometer, we pushed our way carefully along to the highest point of the narrow ridge, in order to mark it with a cairn of rocks. Just as we reached it, the Indian who was still in the lead, suddenly stopped and pointed to the ground. There, on the very summit of Chief Mountain, safely anchored by rocks from the effect of wind or tempest, lay a small, weather beaten bison skull. It was certainly one of the very oldest I have ever seen. Even in the pure air of that mountain top it had rotted away until there was little else than the frontal bone and the stubs on which had been the horns. Billy picked it up and handed it to us quietly, saying with perfect conviction, "The old Flathead's pillow!"

Stimson concluded by noting that they left the skull where they had found it, believing "…that the devotion of the old warrior who had brought it was an influence quite sufficient to protect this memorial of his visit."

Today, the 9,056-foot mountain is not so difficult to ascend. By using J. Gordon Edwards' book, *A Climber's Guide to Glacier National Park*, the

RICK GRAETZ

challenge of route-finding is simplified and, because of a series of dirt roads to the base, a trip up this mountain can be completed in one long day. In fact, rock cairns have been laid out to mark the route all the way to the top. From this vantage many of the park's more spectacular peaks can be seen, as well as the plains stretching beyond the limits of the imagination. Off in this direction can be seen the Sweet Grass Hills and, on a clear day, the Bear Paw Mountains—well beyond a hundred miles distant. Closer, as one looks to the west, is Mt. Merritt, with Old Sun Glacier covering most of its east face. Also to the west can be seen Mt. Cleveland—at 10,438 feet, the highest mountain in the park.

THE CAPTURE OF JOE COSLEY

by R.C. "Bert" Gildart

Above: *Cosley Lake.*
Right: *The Cosley tree bearing initials he is presumed to have cut in the 1920s. This tree received so much attention by visitors that, after it died, the section with his initials was removed and preserved by the Park Service.*

Early in the morning Joe Heimes discovered an illegal cache of furs and, after a hurried trip back to his ranger station to alert others in authority, he returned and settled in behind a large fir tree, determined to wait for the poacher's return.

Six hours later the low clouds that had been hanging over the valley floor began to unleash their load. At times there was rain, other times a mixture of snow and rain. Heimes was getting wet and he was growing very cold.

In another two hours Joe was down to his last cigarette, and even on a miserable day in May the mosquitoes in the back country of Glacier National Park were out in force. Heimes was beginning to get discouraged, afraid the poacher had caught wind of his presence. But Heimes was not one to give up easily, and so he resolved to wait until dark.

Around dusk, Joe's large malamute dog perked up her ears and emitted a low rumbling growl. Clamping a firm hand over its muzzle and unholstering his pistol, Joe began looking around. Suddenly a large raw-boned man entered camp, taking strides, as Joe recalled, "like Bigfoot." Then the lanky man took off his pack, laid down his rifle and began nursing the still-smoldering fire.

"I was half way to him," recalled Joe, "before he heard me. Then he looked up and grabbed for his gun. But I had him dead in my sights, and I hollered, "You lay your hand on that gun and, by God, I'll shoot you right through the guts!"

The man Heimes had caught on that wet spring day in 1929 was no ordinary poacher. His name was Joe Cosley, and his history to that time included the distinction of having been appointed a ranger in 1910 when Glacier became a park, being fired several years later for fur trapping in the park; a WWI record of having killed 60 Germans as a Canadian sniper, and the notoriety of being able to evade both American and Canadian authorities for almost 20 years. "He was," recalled Heimes from his cabin in Lakeside, Montana, "a mountain man who was every bit the equivalent of Kit Carson or Jim Bridger. Luck was all that enabled me to catch him."

Whether it was luck or not is debatable, for Heimes does not appear to have been a man to trifle with. A ranger for 38 years in Glacier National Park, he retired in 1962. But in 1989, his eyes still were piercing, his voice firm, and his hands and back still strong enough to harvest a cord of wood a day. "Though if you want it," said Joe, "it'll cost you $450."

But Joe considered apprehending Cosley to have been luck, which continued and enabled him to march Cosley out from the back country. "Yes, sir," recalled Heimes, "Cosley had a streak of bad luck for a while but only for a short while. Before we were finished with him, I'd say his shrewdness and good luck were back, and in great abundance."

Heimes caught Cosley on May 8 in the Belly River Country of Glacier

INDEPENDENT
JOE COSLEY

Joe Cosley was born May 24, 1870 aboard the cabin sailboat his French father and Algonquin Indian mother used at the time for commercial fishing in Lake Huron. Early years also included life on a homestead in Ontario, Canada with subsequent moves into various parts of the southwestern U.S. At the age of 25, records indicate he was living in Kalispell, Montana and working as a U.S. Forest Service ranger in what is now Glacier National Park.

In 1910 he was transferred from the Forest Service to the Park Service and served as a ranger until he was dismissed for his trapping activities. As Joe Heimes said, "Cosley had one set of rules, the Park Service another."

Even in his early years an aura of mystery surrounded Cosley, and people liked to spin yarns about him, some based on the truth, some probably not. For instance, Joe had many girl friends, but one returned his $1500 diamond ring to him. Cosley is reputed to have buried the ring in a tree and then told others of this action. For a while there were diamond ring prospectors peeling away new growth bark in many areas of the park.

Another legend about Cosley concerns his illegal trapping experiences and, once, when two tired rangers were attempting to overtake Cosley, they were surprised when he suddenly appeared from the brush. He said he knew they would be tired and invited them to join him for supper, where he served a delicious French stew.

Another time, in what may have been a more characteristic fashion, Cosley stated simply to a ranger that if he ever caught him on the trail again he'd kill him.

Cosley's career also included a stint in WWI with the Canadian Army, by whom he was decorated for his skills as a sniper. Today, Glacier honors the man with a namesake: Cosley Lake is located between Belly River Ranger Station and Stoney Indian Pass, one of the most beautiful areas of Glacier National Park.

Cosley's primary source of income, however, was always his trapping, and in this mode he met his demise in September 1944. At the age of 73, in a wind-swept trapper cabin north of Prince Albert, he died alone of scurvy. The last entry into his log reads:

"I am growing weaker. I can hardly write…I have reached the end."

MONTANA HISTORICAL SOCIETY

Joe Heimes in the 1980s.

National Park, a place where winter reluctantly releases its grip on the land. Snow still blanketed the hills and formed white patches across the meadow. "I was preparing for John J. Wes to bring in my spring supplies," recalled Heimes, "and I had to blow a beaver dam which was backing snow melt up over the old wagon road. Wes would come in through Cardston and Mountain View with a Canadian Mounted Police escort in an old wagon and each year the trail flooded for miles. I had to blow that dam away twice a year.

"Well, at any rate, that's when I saw tracks down there in the snow and the sand, and I could see where someone had been looking around for beaver. My dog and I followed a long way and finally we came to a tarp laying over a pole. Inside, there was a hindquarter of beaver, and a muskrat was stuck between his blankets along with several traps. When I saw that we went back to the ranger station at Belly River where I called Tom Whitcraft, the ranger then at Waterton Ranger Station. He wasn't there but the Canadians said they'd tell him he was urgently needed—and precisely where I could be found. Then, mighty quick, we hiked the three miles back to the poacher's camp and hid behind a tree.

"As I said, we waited almost ten full hours before he showed and I caught him. But at the time I wasn't sure who I'd caught. I'd never even seen a picture of him before. But I'd heard a description, so when he gave me a fake name I said, 'Well, you sure look more like Joe Cosley to me'."

"Glaring back, he said, 'Well, I'm Joe Cosley all right, but you ain't taking me in.' And then he added, 'Ain't no ranger in this park takin' me in.'

"You know, I might have let him go if he hadn't said that. I didn't want to go to headquarters anyway, I had a dog team and it meant I might be gone a week. It was too much work. And back in those days poaching wasn't a real serious thing. Generally, we'd just take the furs, unload their gun and let them go. As it was, I spent three long days with the man, not to mention what happened after the trial.

"The first night after I caught him we were too far from the station to go back. The woods were thick, and it was almost dark. So we stayed up all night. We just sat there watching each other. And every 15 minutes or so he'd tell me he had to go to the bathroom.

"It was a long night, but finally morning came and Cosley said, 'Well, you might be going but I shore ain't.' I told him then that I'd cut a stick and beat him back to the station, and that just as soon as I finished the smoke he'd given

me, we were going. That convinced him, but we hadn't gone over 300 feet when all at once he took off running. Never said 'Goodbye' or nothing.

"Well in '29 I wasn't so bad at running myself, so I took off after him and tackled him. Cosley took a few swings but he wasn't really fighting, just more trying to get away. Finally, he gave up and said, 'Okay, I'll go now.'

"Well, we hadn't gone another 300 feet and I had to make another flying tackle. After wrestling him to the ground he said, 'Okay, I'll go.'

"This happened one more time. Only this time he was fighting for keeps; I was afraid he'd kill me. But finally I had the opportunity to take his head and bang it against a tree. Down he went. I tied him with the laces of my boots.

"When Cosley came to, he said, 'I can't go; I'm sick.' Well, I knew he was sick, damn sick and at that point I didn't know what I was going to do. But just then my dog's ears perked up and along came Tom Whitcraft and the Canadian I'd left the message with. Just like the Seventh Cavalry they were, arriving in the nick of time. We walked the rest of the way back to the station, and we had no more trouble with Cosley that day.

"Next day Tom said he wanted to go back to Waterton and I said the hell with that. You see, Tom was a good looking fellow and," emphasized Joe with a twinkle in his eye, "a real woman chaser. In fact, that's the reason I couldn't get ahold of him the first day. He was single then and he'd been chasin' a woman. So I said, 'You're going to let me take this bird over Gable Pass myself? My God, if Cosley gets away then I'm in trouble and you will be too.' That changed his mind!"

For Heimes, the remainder of the trip to court was without incident. A grueling trip on snow shoes over Gable Pass to East Glacier and then, a day later, a train trip to what is now West Glacier. Then the next day a trial began about two o'clock in the afternoon. Cosley was fined $100 and given a suspended jail sentence of 90 days. He was then released. And that, reflected Heimes, is when Cosley's usual good luck returned.

"What they should have done is made him spend at least five days in jail. That would have given us a chance to beat him back to look for all those hides he had cached. As it was I went over to a store in Belton (now West Glacier) and store owner Mark Sibley said, 'You know where Cosley is now?' I said no, and that I didn't give a damn just so long as Cosley stays out of my way, that I wanted to stay out of his way too!

"Mark said, 'Well, he's on his way back to Belly River, and he's just left. He's going to try and beat you guys back to his beaver cache!'"

"As soon as I heard that I went to see this fellow up at McDonald Station by the name of Clarence Willy. Willy took right off after Cosley and Willy was a good man, a good strong fellow. He followed Cosley 12 to 15 miles but returned late that night and said that Cosley was a little too good a traveler for him.

"Next morning Tom Whitcraft and I took the train back to East Glacier and then drove a Model T by way of Cardston to the Canadian Belly River Station. From there we had to walk, but we weren't too concerned. It was about 30 miles from the town of Belton to Belly River and today that takes a good strong hiker about two days. And that's if he's on good summer-cleared trails!

BRUCE SELYEM   JOHN REDDY

"But when we got back to his camp all we found were tracks. During the course of the night, that 59-year-old man had snowshoed up McDonald and Mineral Creeks, crossed over Ahern Pass and removed 40 to 50 beaver blankets and somehow disappeared from the Belly River Country. We couldn't have missed Cosley by more than a few hours. Maybe only minutes. What luck! But to this day you know, I'm not sure whether it was his good luck or my good luck. You see, after that he went north into Canada where I've been told he trapped, wrote old girl friends and became quite a legend.

"But me, I never saw the man again."

Joe Heimes went northeast when he was a young man—from California to Shelby, Montana, riding the rails for the sole purpose of seeing the Jack Dempsey-Tommy Gibbons fight. That was in June of 1923 and, at the time, Heimes was 22 years old.

Heimes stayed for the fight held July 4 and spent much time prior to the fight talking to the two pugilists. His scrapbook contained posed pictures of both Dempsey and Gibbons, which Joe took himself.

After the fight, Heimes went to Glacier and, as fate would have it, an appropriate job was waiting for just such a man as Joe. It was the beginning of a career with the Park Service that lasted until 1962, when he retired as a National Park Service ranger.

Although never married, Heimes has pictures of a number of women in his scrapbook, most of whom, said his friends, were the nicest things you'd ever want to meet. "And they'd ride, walk—even run—to the most remote spots in the park to see him." Today, his companion is a malamute dog that is very much like the one he had with him in the Belly River Country that eventful day of 1929.

Heimes' experiences were varied and fascinating, but the one that received the most publicity is his encounter with Joe Cosley. In the mid-1990s, Heimes was still employed, working as a caretaker near Lakeside, Montana.

Above: *Atop Ahern Pass, over which 59-year-old Joe Cosley raced on snowshoes to beat officials to his illegal cache of pelts. This view is toward Helen Lake.*
Left: *Cosley Ridge.*

43

Ranger's Notebook

by R.C. "Bert" Gildart

"Where can I go now and view nature undisturbed?"
John James Audubon, 1846

Late one evening in Glacier's Belly River country, I watched with a small group of companions as a herd of about 20 elk materialized from the woods and slowly grouped along the stream that ran by our camp. For more than an hour the herd meandered along the bank, stopping here and there to quench their thirst. Now and then a calf would kick up its heels and charge through the water.

Suddenly an old bull lifted his head and flicked his ears back and forth—testing the air and trying to locate sounds inaudible to human ears. Then, gradually, we too heard the noise; a sharp crack from the woods that grew louder and louder as the unidentified object moved closer.

The sound of breaking twigs sent the herd galloping across the stream, churning up water as they trotted across the shallows. Then, just as suddenly as they had materialized, they were gone, disappearing into the rapidly descending gloom of night.

Next morning at the crack of dawn, our curiosities aroused, we ambled down to the bank where our elk had been drinking and found tracks made by what appeared from the sign to have been a small black bear. Nothing really dramatic, but, nevertheless, a reminder that we had seen something special—something that one generally sees only in the wilderness.

My companions and I have had many similar experiences in our years of wandering through Glacier's back country. Once it was a cow elk swimming across Lincoln Lakes; another time it was a porcupine rubbing its quills along the side of our tent during some wee hour of the morning. The point is that it's still possible to enjoy experiences that John James Audubon was searching back in 1846. We can have these opportunities primarily because Congress decreed in 1916 that a number of areas would be set aside as "vignettes of our National Heritage." Because of a superb system of trails, Glacier is one park that offers easy access to its wilderness areas. Venture along one of them and invariably you will return with indelible memories to savor for years.

GLACIER TRAILS

Visitors arriving in Glacier for the first time often find it disconcerting as they begin their attempt to plan a back-country trip into the park. Their dilemma is understandable; most of the park's trails are one-way trails that leave hikers miles from their points of origin. There are, however, several trails that traverse some of the most superb country the park has to offer—without leaving one stranded at the end. These are the park's loop trails, and several are described below. Also included are two other excursions that could round out the hiker's appreciation of the park. **For easy access, all areas will be named according to their point of origin.**

All of the following hikes are strenuous ones. They should not be attempted by anyone who is not in good physical condition. Carry along water from a known clean source, or a stove, so that water can be boiled. Additionally, in most areas, open fires are not permitted, necessitating possession of a good backpack stove. Because special park regulations may apply and the number of visitors permitted into these back-country areas at any one time is limited, it is mandatory that hikers register at either a visitor center or a ranger station.

HINKE/SACILOTTO

JOHN WINNIE, JR.

TRAILS

Packer's Roost

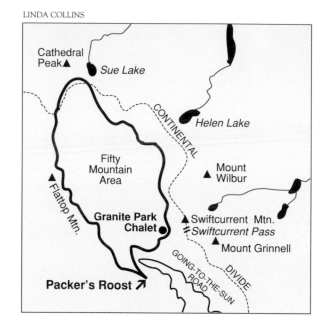

This 32-mile, three- to four-day round trip hike offers special views of the peaks of the Lewis and Livingstone ranges. In midsummer a pageant of wildflowers greets the hiker. So might grizzly and black bears. This is prime habitat for bears as well as for goats, marmots, pikas and deer, the last of which may wander through your campground.

The trail begins at Packer's Roost. Two miles later it crosses McDonald Creek via a suspension bridge that usually is in place by the first week in June. Several miles later the trail climbs 1,800 feet to the heights of Flattop Mountain. A campground is located here along the west bank of Flattop Creek. As with many park campgrounds, it offers a privy, food cache pole and hitchrack. Because of the steep climb, hikers should spend their first night here.

The distance from Flattop Mountain to Fifty Mountain is 12 miles. The trip continues along Flattop Mountain with very little elevation gain. At the north end of Flattop Mountain, the trail drops 600 feet into the Kipp Creek Drainage, then climbs abruptly to the Fifty Mountain Campground, located in one of the most beautiful sections of the entire park.

From Fifty Mountain, one returns along the Highline Trail, so named because it generally maintains an elevation above timberline. From the campground it is 12 miles to the Granite Park area, one of the park's two back-country "hotels." Make reservations to spend the night—the amenities offered are worth the cost. Naturalist talks are given in the evening, and occasionally one can see bears from the balcony. If the $35 to $40 cost is prohibitive, hikers still are welcome to refresh themselves with tea or another nonalcoholic beverage.

Besides the chalet, visitors can choose a nearby campground. From the Granite Park area, you must hike a total of about seven miles—virtually all downhill—to return to your point of origin.

Left: *Mount Grinnell from near Granite Park.*
Far left: *Small Creek, near Ahern Pass.*

Facing page: *Moonrise over Mt. Cannon, as seen from near Packer's Roost.*

47

Two Medicine Camp-ground

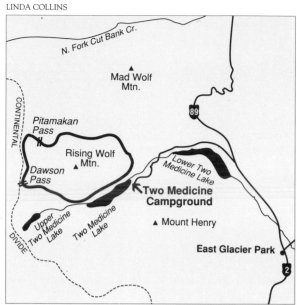

Above: Icebergs in August on a high mountain lake in Glacier.

Right: Studying the beargrass.

Facing page: Two Medicine Lake.

A strenuous 17.4-mile round trip that is best enjoyed by allowing two or three days. The suggested route for this hike is in a clockwise direction starting from Two Medicine Lake and continuing to Pitamakan Pass. This trail may not be open until early July. Because of the precipitous nature of the trail between Dawson and Pitamakan passes, horses are not permitted; persons suffering from acrophobia should beware.

In addition to unsurpassed panoramic views offered by the lofty passes, this area offers abundant opportunities to see goats and sheep. In the lower elevations, bears occasionally are seen. From the trail near Pitamakan Pass, two small lakes at the head of Cut Bank Valley are visible. Frozen over until midsummer, they are dotted with icebergs that may linger in the mountain's shadows throughout summer. Two back-country campsites are present and are located adjacent to lakes that at times offer excellent opportunities for the angler. One of these is No Name Lake, the other Oldman Lake. Because wood fires are not permitted, a backpack stove is recommended.

48

JOHN REDDY

Bowman Lake

LINDA COLLINS

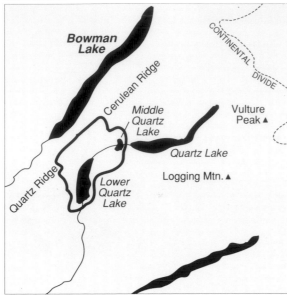

ABOVE: RICK GRAETZ; BELOW: ED WOLFE

A strenuous 13-mile round trip that can be broken up by camping at either Lower Quartz Lake or Quartz Lake. Anglers should try for cutthroat and dolly varden trout. The hike passes through a dense forest, which is one of the main reasons for venturing into this drainage. From Quartz Lake there are excellent views of Vulture Peak straddling the Continental Divide. A quartz vein on Vulture Peak at the headwaters of Quartz Creek contains a small vein of copper ore that stimulated a bit of unsuccessful prospecting after its discovery in 1876.

This is prime grizzly bear habitat, so proper disposal of trash and fish entrails is essential.

Hikers interested in this trip should be prepared to negotiate wet and boggy spots. They should also be in good shape. The trail climbs 1,100 feet over Quartz Ridge, then drops to Lower Quartz Lake. There is another 1,000-foot climb over Cerulean Ridge returning from Middle Quartz Lake to Bowman Lake.

Left: *Vulture Peak.*
Below: *Cutthroat trout from Glacier country.*

Facing page: *Bowman Lake.*

Right: *Fireweed.*

Facing page: *In a meadow near Poia Lake at sunrise.*

TRAILS

Grinnell Glacier Exhibit near Appekunny Creek

This is a round trip that will leave you only two miles from your car when the trail terminates at the Many Glacier Campground store. The total length of the trip is about 25 miles depending on whether the recommended side trip is included in your hiking itinerary. Highlights of this trip include fishing for arctic grayling at both Poia and Elizabeth lakes and for rainbow trout at Kennedy Creek.

Before the completion of Ptarmigan Tunnel in 1931, the trail over Red Gap Pass was the direct connection with the Belly River area. Today this trail joins with the one from Ptarmigan Tunnel about two miles from Elizabeth Lake. Dropping down into this lake is well worth the time; the scenery is spectacular and the fishing at times can be excellent.

Two camp areas are located along this route, one at Poia Lake, the other at both the foot and head of Elizabeth Lake. Fires are permitted at both campsites, although it is often difficult to obtain wood. Only wood that is dead and down can be used, so it is advisable to carry a stove.

Recommended time for this trip is three days. The trail is steep and rises 2,700 feet to reach Red Gap Pass. Just prior to reaching the pass, one must negotiate a series of extremely steep switchbacks. A similar drop in elevation to Elizabeth Lake includes another series of switchbacks.

The climb from Elizabeth Lake to Ptarmigan Tunnel is 2,300 feet. From the tunnel the trail is downhill all the way to Swiftcurrent Campstore. Backpacks could be left here (at owner's risk), while hikers trudge the last two miles along the paved road back to their car.

PAT O'HARA

Right: *The view from Swiftcurrent Peak.*

Facing page: *Red Rock Falls, ultimately a product of Red Rock Lake.*

54

Swift-current Lodge

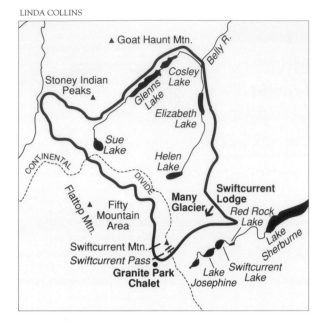

LINDA COLLINS

PAT O'HARA

This round-trip hike traverses a route that is a historic one in the annals of the park.

Historically the route is referred to as the North Circle route and was initiated in 1915 by W.N. Noffsinger, an attorney from Kalispell, who began the Park Saddle Horse Company. Under the –X6 (Bar X Six) brand, the company expanded until it owned more than 1,000 head of horses, making it the largest saddle horse outfit of its kind in the world. Each year the company served more than 10,000 park visitors, and it did so successfully until World War II. After the war, the "discovery" of the Going-to-the-Sun Road by a more affluent car-owning American society ended the saddle horse business.

The North Circle trip, one of the company's most popular, required five days, with stops at tent camps or chalets. Today, the following suggested route is identical to the one traversed by riders bouncing along on Bar X Six stock between 1915 and 1942.

Begin your trip at the Swiftcurrent Lodge located in the Many Glacier Valley. Stops may include overnight camping at Elizabeth Lake, Belly River, Cosley Lake, Stoney Indian Lake, Goat Haunt, Fifty Mountain and Granite Park Chalet. On the last day you will hike over Swiftcurrent Pass, traveling beneath the Swiftcurrent fire lookout and then Red Rock Lake prior to concluding your trip some four to seven days later back at Swiftcurrent Lodge.

This trip is an arduous one as it passes through the heart of the park and crosses the Continental Divide several times. Excellent fishing for several species of trout including arctic grayling can be had along the way.

DOUG DYE

Above: *Boulder Pass and Hole-in-the-Wall during the 1988 forest fires.*
Right: *Thimbleberry.*

Facing page: *Upper Kintla Lake and Boulder Peak.*

NEAL & MARY JANE MISHLER

56

LINDA COLLINS

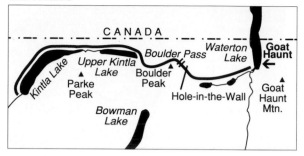

TRAILS

Goat Haunt to Lower Kintla Lake

This 32-mile, one-way hike is one of the most rewarding trips for the experienced backpacker. It offers a variety of terrain and traverses deep, forested valleys, lakes, glacial cirques and two mountain passes. Because the trail passes through all the park's vegetative zones, the opportunity exists to see virtually all species of park wildlife.

Boulder Pass is the higher of the two passes. Fewer than 50 years ago, the basin on the east side of the pass was filled by massive Boulder Glacier. Today only small patches of ice on the north slopes of Boulder Peak remain. Still, striated rocks, sharp moraines and melted lakes abound, providing mute testimony to glacial activity.

Subalpine larch, the Glacier Park tree, also is found in this vicinity, and, appropriately, its presence also is associated with the recent glacial activity. Look for these interesting trees near Boulder Pass. They are characterized by needles that grow 20 to 40 to a bundle and measure one to two inches long. Unlike most conifers, the larch sheds its needles in the fall. The altitudinal range of this species serves as the best distinction from its close relative, the western larch. Subalpine larch grows only in partially sheltered areas at or near treeline, many hundreds of feet above the uppermost limits of western larch. Elevation and the wooly character of the new branch shoots are the most reliable distinguishing features.

In some years, snow remains on or along the trail throughout the summer, particularly in the Boulder Pass area. Because the trail in this area traverses much rock and scree, hikers should be alert for rock cairns that mark the way.

After leaving the Boulder Pass area, the trail drops sharply into the Kintla Valley where it winds through luxuriant growths of cow-parsnip and thimbleberry. These plants can make hiking difficult—particularly on a wet day. Foul weather gear is highly recommended.

A number of campgrounds are placed along the entire route, but, if possible, try to spend one night at the Hole-in-the-Wall Campground. Because of surrounding waterfalls, the location is particularly enchanting.

The only drawback of the entire trip is logistics. Transportation must be arranged, as Kintla Lake Campground lies at the end of an unimproved dirt road—well over 150 miles from Goat Haunt. Nevertheless, the drive takes you through several remote and historical sections of the park, providing additional intrigue to the overall trip. As a last resort, rest up and retrace your steps. As with all of Glacier's trails, repeating a hike invariably offers a new set of experiences.

JOHN REDDY

HOWIE WOLKE

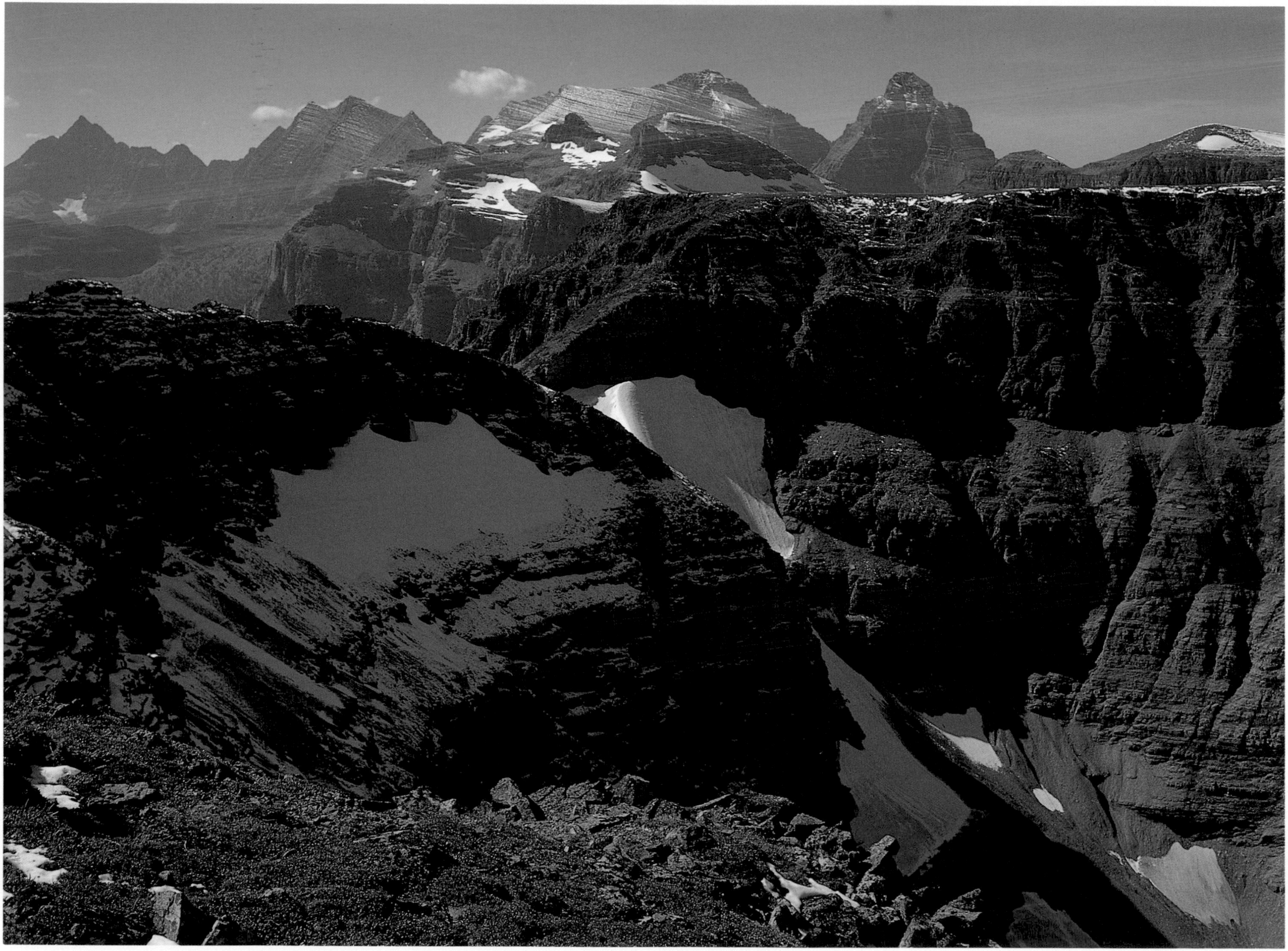

Above: The view of Thunderbird Mountain from Hole-in-the-Wall.
Left: Kayaking on Kintla Lake.
Far left: Long Knife Creek in the Kintla area.

Facing page: View of Noma, Peabody, Kintla and Kinnerly peaks from Chapman Peak ridge near Hole-in-the-Wall.

59

JOHN REDDY

Valleys of Southwest Glacier Park

The southwest corner of the park is wilderness in the true sense of the word. It can be thought of as an extension of the Great Bear Wilderness to the south. Although trails exist, they receive only intermittent maintenance, if they receive it at all. The route east through Nyack Creek across Cut Bank, Dawson and other passes is historic as well as scenic. It was much frequented by Indians traveling to and from buffalo country.

Hikers have an additional measure of freedom in this area. Although permits are required, as they are throughout the park, backpackers are not confined to designated campgrounds. Hiking is strenuous at certain times of the year because of damp, thick, brushy undergrowth. Keep in mind that this is prime bear country.

No specific hikes are outlined here since routes are easy to identify up the Lincoln, Harrison, Nyack, Coal, Park and Ole creek drainages.

Above: *Rafting the Middle Fork of the Flathead.*
Left: *Ferns and vine in a damp and shady Glacier National Park creek bottom.*

Facing page: *Middle Fork of the Flathead River.*

Right: *North Fork of the Flathead River near Nyack.*

Facing page:
Mt. St. Nicholas from U.S. Highway 2.

Right: *Skiers on Going-to-the-Sun Road above Lake McDonald, with Mt. Cannon in the background.*

Facing page: *A February sunset in the park.*

SKI TOURS IN GLACIER PARK

Virgin snow lay all around as we skied down the gentle slope of a winding trail and glided slowly onto the white mantle covering Josephine Lake. Here, my partner and I were reminded of the first commandment for skiers in Glacier National Park, "Be thou alert to change."

Several minutes later, as we rested in the middle of one of the park's frozen waterways, we noticed that the temperature was rising fast. Every gust of wind now seemed to carry an ominous message: Mother Nature was not to be calmed!

Half an hour ago, the cold wind had been intense enough to drive a throbbing pain into our heads. Now, well past the center of the lake, it was too warm to ski wrapped in our down parkas. Our thermometer indicated the temperature was beginning to stabilize near 40 degrees, an increase of more than 45 degrees in the past two hours from the overnight low.

After we made the far shore, we began changing wax, and, as we did, we watched the wind whipping snow between our feet and off the surrounding mountain peaks, snow not yet compacted by the warm sun and wind.

Then Mother Nature growled!

Along the far ridge a dull roar began and soon filled the air. The mountains seemed to groan from every direction with such a vehemence that it was difficult to audibly locate the exact source of the disturbance. Our sight, however, was not deceived and, from Grinnell Peak, we saw large slabs of snow sliding down the peak and out onto Josephine Lake, where we had just labored. Huge boulders were cascading down the slope; dwarfed trees were being upended. Then just as quickly as it began, all motion ceased, the roar abated, and gusts at Josephine Lake were again audible.

Philosophizing as much to myself as to seasonal park ranger Fred Reese, I said, "Fred, for once we chose the right path!"

Every year in some part of the country, including Glacier Park, winter enthusiasts are killed or maimed because of an unfamiliarity with their surroundings. It need not be so.

An appreciation of the snow conditions, an understanding of winter trails, or a realistic analysis of their skills could have averted disaster. Such knowledge can enable the skier to prepare adequately for a unique tour through Glacier during quite possibly the most fascinating season of all.

Unstable weather conditions, a prime contributor to avalanches, are not at all uncommon in Glacier. At times, temperatures may plummet to 20 or 30 below and then, several days later, warm winds or "chinooks" may send the mercury soaring into the 40s or even higher, in the course of several hours. The result is unstable snow conditions, which precipitate numerous avalanches throughout the park. The important thing, then, is to recognize the danger signs.

Above: A snowbound
Granite Park Chalet.

Facing page: Stanton
Mountain and Going-
to-the-Sun Road.

that they rely on skins for climbing and for "kick" over flat terrain. A downhill wax then serves for any coasting.

Because many of the trails over which you may wish to ski in Glacier are steep and narrow, and often prove difficult to negotiate, it may be in your best interest to remove your skis and carry them over these areas. To permit freedom of motion for your arms, a backpack or rucksack that has attachments for packing skis is a real convenience. If you slip, your hands are free for recovery; your skis are secure and won't slip away as you reach to regain balance.

Because the terrain in Glacier can be rough on equipment, one precautionary measure that should be taken is to include a spare tip and extra cable, especially for trips longer than just a few miles. If you are accompanied by other skiers—as you should be for safety's sake—and, if you are using the same brand of equipment, a smaller number of total spare parts may be carried by the entire group. This practice is used by patrol rangers and should not be overlooked, as you would testify had you ever floundered back through several feet of powder with a broken binding.

Prudence dictates investigating local weather reports at park headquarters. Some skiers even include a small transistor radio for trail-side forecasts. The weather man is often wrong, which is understandable when talking about an area whose weather is determined by coastal and continental weather fronts and huge elevation differences. If he predicted "blue skies and light zephyrs ahead" better prepare for a white-out or a prolonged blizzard. Should you be in the back country at such an inopportune time, it would be wise not to travel. Better to lose time and remain snug in your sturdy mountain tent than to risk fatigue, hypothermia or the prospect of stumbling off a cliff. Prepare for such a stopover by including extra food, enough for two or three days.

If you are caught in a sudden storm or plan to camp above timberline, you will appreciate having a self-supporting tent. Locating logs in high country to serve as anchors or "deadmen" for tent ropes and pegs is an impossibility, and snow depth is so great that pegs are ineffective.

With the thousands of miles of trails available during the summer, one of the most difficult decisions to be made by the winter vagabond is where to go in this 1,538-square-mile park. Further complicating matters is the fact that a number of summer highways now remain unplowed and provide excellent opportunities to see Glacier by ski during the winter. In one such unplowed area, for instance, Fred Reese and I encountered a mountain lion that had been following a herd of elk. The story of its stalk was recorded in the snow. But not all roads will provide this wonderful opportunity. In some areas, snowmobilers have free rein.

Avalanche Lake—Perhaps one of the most rewarding short jaunts is to Avalanche Lake, located west of the Continental Divide. To reach your starting point, drive along the Going-to-the-Sun Road around Lake McDonald until you come to the unplowed section. Now, continue along this famed highway—but not on skis—for about the next four miles depending on how far the road has been plowed. Soon, if you do not spend too much time photographing frozen McDonald Falls, you will come to Avalanche Campground. Avalanche Lake is then two and a half miles straight up a winding

In some areas of the country, the Forest Service is helping those interested by offering free courses in snow study. Prior to skiing in Glacier, take one if possible—otherwise, write a Forest Service office such as the one located at the Federal Building, Missoula, Montana 59801 and ask for the brochure on avalanches. Study this pamphlet thoroughly. If you follow its cautions, you should be able to avoid dangerous situations.

Unstable snow conditions also produce complicated and uncommon waxing problems. Waxing gear should run almost the entire gamut. Thus your pack should include the klisters, and a small torch to remove this messy paste if temperatures suddenly drop. Many have found waxing to be such a chore

DOUG DYE

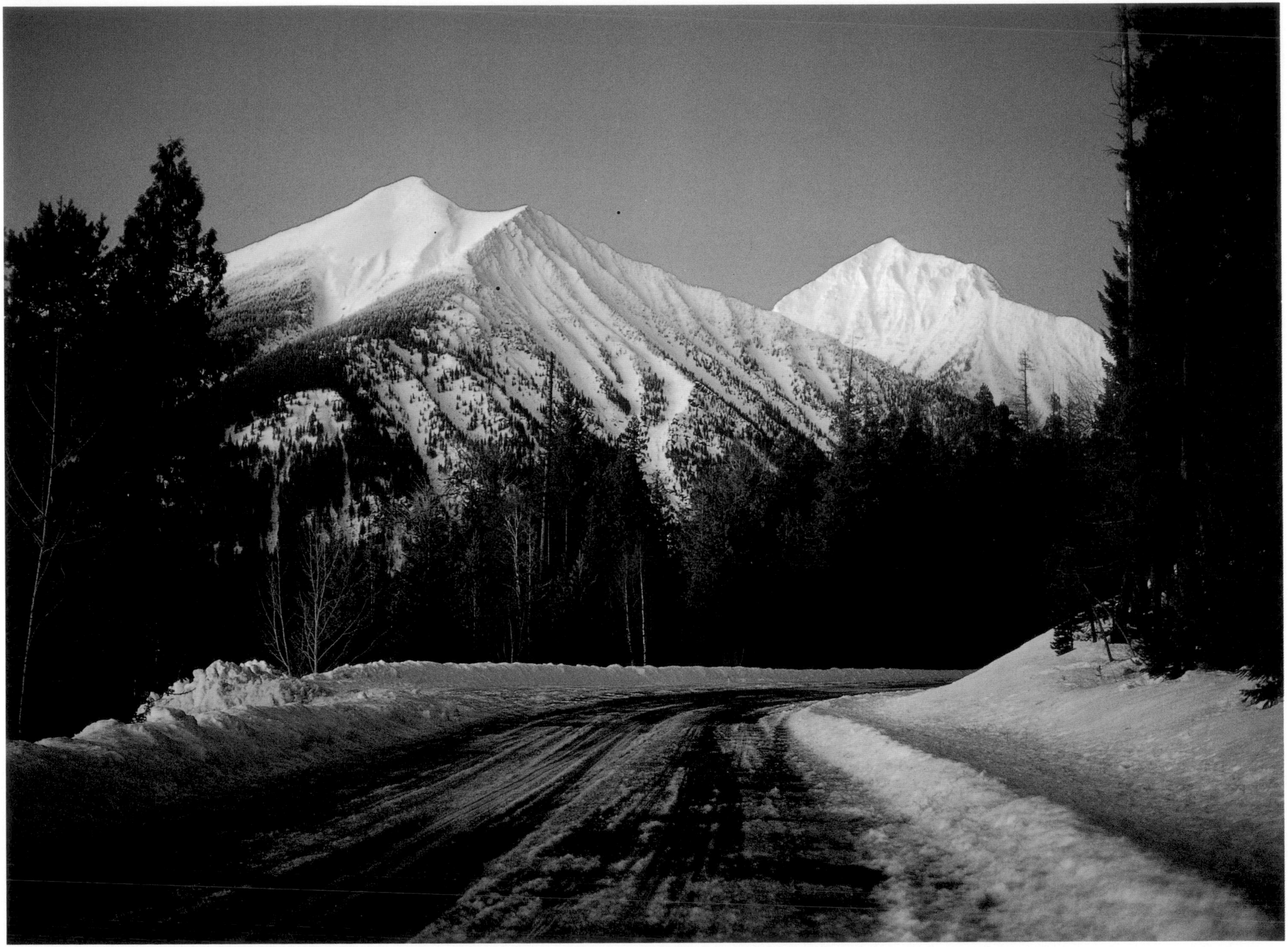

Right: *Bighorn sheep.*

Facing page: *Enjoying Glacier's snow and its ice.*

TOM J. ULRICH

DAN HELTERLINE

trail. At times, even skins won't provide a firm grip and you will have to remove your skis. But the view of the gorge is worth the effort, and there is always the opportunity to observe deer and elk. The area is also one of the few within the park in which I have seen mountain lions.

Because this lake, always frozen during the winter, is located in a lofty cirque, the surrounding mountains often are shrouded by clouds. If you make this a two-day winter trip and camp at the lake, you can intimately view the wilderness surrounding this frozen expanse. Regardless of the number of days used, the skiing time, depending on conditions, is about eight hours.

Many Glacier—East of the Continental Divide, the probability of finding clear skies is better than on the west side. One excellent trip that could conceivably be made in two days is to ski into the Many Glacier area. Three to five days would make a more relaxed and enjoyable trip. To reach the Many Glacier area, drive from the town of Babb to the Many Glacier entrance station. At this point, if the road is unplowed—to be expected—you will then have to ski 10 miles along a flat surface to reach Many Glacier. Once there, you will have an unexcelled opportunity to photograph bighorn sheep. This is the wintering area for these mountain monarchs, and in November and December you probably will see and hear them as they collide with one another and shatter the silence locked in this immense valley.

Josephine and Grinnell Lakes; Advanced Trips—Another excellent ski-tour in the Many Glacier area is to Josephine and Grinnell lakes. You will find the trailhead for this trip near the end of Swiftcurrent Lake. Round-trip time will require about five hours, but skiing across these lakes to view snow plumes trailing away from lofty mountain peaks is well worth the energy expended; it will long be one of my most memorable experiences.

I would also recommend other parts of the park for their unique beauty. Accessibility, however, is more difficult, and advice on entrance into these areas is best obtained locally. Prior to your arrival, order a topographical map

from the Glacier Park Historical Society and then discuss one of the following treks with a park ranger:

From Chief Mountain to Belly River and Elizabeth Lake; from St. Mary to Red Eagle Lake; from Summit, between East Glacier and Walton Ranger Station, out Autumn Creek; and from the Loop, above Avalanche Campground, to Granite Park Chalet. (This last route is best attempted in May, after the main road has been partially opened.)

As in the two areas previously discussed, avalanche danger in these latter basins does not constitute a major hazard. All these trails are suitable for any who are in good physical condition and have a reasonable knowledge of how to camp during the winter.

Glacier's Heartland: Waterton to Packer's Roost—There is one final area that I would recommend, but with some reservations. This trek is a minor odyssey and should not be attempted unless you have a sophisticated knowledge of winter survival, are in excellent physical condition and have plenty of time.

On this trip, you will ski through the very heart of the park, where some of the loftiest mountains in Montana serve as sentinels. Here, as you leave the valleys behind and approach one of the summits, you will find no other sign of life, save perhaps a ptarmigan or a gaping hole left in the snow by a startled grouse that had been seeking relief from the biting wind. This area, as some have said, is truly the "Crown of the Continent," but it is also a region that welcomes no one.

Prior to embarking, analyze your skills objectively, and by all means, go well out of your way to avoid slopes that even hint at avalanche potential. In December 1970 six men lost their lives in a snow slide while attempting a winter assault on nearby Mt. Cleveland, Glacier's highest peak.

To begin this trip through Glacier's heartland—best made between January and April—drive to Waterton townsite in Canada, where you should advise one of the Canadian park wardens (rangers) of your intentions. Generally, you may say that your route will take you around Waterton Lake, down Waterton Valley and then up several thousand feet to Fifty Mountain. From here you will want to cut across country passing over Flattop Mountain, dropping into the Mineral Creek drainage and coming out finally near Packer's Roost. Allow about five days to cover this trek of approximately 35 miles.

Return transportation to Canada, or to the foot of McDonald Lake if you decide to reverse the route, will have to be arranged in advance. Usually this necessitates either renting a car or arriving with your companions in two vehicles.

Logistics, though, are a minor problem; your greatest difficulty will be selecting one of the almost equally enticing areas through which to ski. But whichever you choose, prepare properly and, upon completion, you'll be fit to try another route…and another.

Well, why not?

Time is in your favor, for in many years you can ski-tour Glacier for almost nine full months.

Left: Snowshoe prints in a moonlit pattern.

Facing page, left: Along the trail, with Mt. Cannon in the distance.

Right: Fresh water is everywhere in winter, but it's not instant.

71

WHAT ABOUT
THE BEARS?

Question: How do you tell the difference between a grizzly bear and a black bear?

Answer: Kick the bear in the rump and climb a tree. If the bear climbs up after you, it's a black bear. If it knocks the tree down, it's a grizzly.

—*Very early bear research method*

One feature that immediately separates black bears and grizzly bears is their temperament. Where one is inclined to be docile, the other is aggressive. Where one retreats, the other advances. And where one climbs trees, the other charges. Paleontologists tell us that it is this skill—the ability to climb trees—that accounts for their dispositions.

From fossil remains it is believed that grizzly bears first emerged about 1 million years ago. *Ursus americanus,* or our now relatively retiring black bear, preceded the grizzly by about another 1 million years. Both animals, however, evolved from common ancestral species, *Ursus etruscus,* with subsequent environmental factors shaping the two distinct personalities.

Above: *Springtime snack for a black bear cub.*

Facing page: *Sunrise in the Many Glacier area, prime bear country.*

73

Right: *The grizzly bear, North America's largest carnivore.*

Facing page: *Hidden Lake is grizzly country.*

Ursus etruscus originally lived in Asian forests. But climatic changes required some bears to evolve into animals of the tundra to cope with the lack of cover. No longer could the tundra bear retreat from danger by taking to the trees, or protect its offspring by sending them into high branches. Instead, to survive attacks from other predators, it became more aggressive. On the treeless prairie, sows were forced to defend their cubs. Assisting them were genetic and evolutionary adaptations such as long claws (useless for climbing trees) and a large physical stature. Huge back muscles evolved for digging up sod in search of underground-dwelling rodents and the roots, tubers and bulbs of plants associated with the plains. Those same back muscles make up the prominent shoulder hump of the modern grizzly.

Where black bear sows retreated from danger, *Ursus arctos*, the evolved grizzly, advanced toward it, and this characteristic was firmly imprinted on the cubs. Not surprisingly, most grizzly bear attacks today involve mothers with their cubs.

The black bear preceded the grizzly to North America, across the periodic land bridge connecting America and Asia, by almost 250,000 years.

Today, the grizzly bear is the largest carnivore in North America. Its family includes the big brown, giant Alaska and the Barren Ground bears. The very largest of these are found in southwestern Alaska, on Kodiak Island. Bears have been killed there that measured nine feet two inches from the tips of their noses to the ends of their short tails. One taken on Kodiak Island weighed an incredible 1,656 pounds. In Glacier, bears are not nearly this big—the largest averages about 600 pounds.

Despite its enormous bulk, the grizzly is surprisingly agile. On the straightaway, bears are fast and have great endurance. A grizzly in Yellowstone Park, running ahead of an automobile, was clocked at 30 miles an hour.

Bears gorge themselves all fall and attain their greatest weight in October just before their long winter sleep.

Bears do not hibernate, although they do den up and spend the winter in a lethargic sleep. The bears usually dig their winter dens in early fall, most of them on north-facing slopes, beneath big tree roots at high elevations. With the onset of the season's first big snowstorm, bears retire to their dens and sleep.

During this long winter sleep, a bear's body temperature drops six to eight degrees, and its heartbeat and breath rate slow down markedly. Unlike the true hibernators, the bear easily can be awakened.

Most bears in Glacier come out of hibernation in April. Shortly after emerging, bears are active, and if food is scarce they lose much of their excess body weight. This is the season when they break into cabins in the North Fork country of Glacier Park.

Bears breed in June and, at such times, the males fight viciously for possession of the females. When dominance has been established and the lesser bear driven from the area, the female and remaining male become very playful. Their courtship lasts for a week or more. After mating, the male wanders off to seek another receptive female.

Cubs are born in January, while the female is in the winter den. Twins are usual, but triplets are common, and occasionally quadruplets occur. At birth

Right: *Only a cub, always a grizzly.*

Facing page: *Lake McDonald.*

the cubs are covered with short gray hair, and their eyes and ears are sealed. The grizzly cub is eight to 10 inches long and weighs from eight ounces to one pound.

Mother bears are strict disciplinarians. The cub that does not heed its mother's command is given a swat that sends it sprawling. The cubs stay with their mother until they are two years old, which means that most females breed only every third year.

Grizzlies rarely climb trees, even as cubs. After a year or two, their claws lose so much curvature that they are not efficient hooks for digging into tree trunks. But there are always exceptions: a bear climbed high into a tree after several hikers near Elizabeth Lake in September 1980.

How dangerous is the grizzly to man? Occasionally human beings are terribly mauled or even killed by these bears. The bodies are seldom eaten, but there are exceptions to this too, and 1980 marked another one of those rare incidents. Again at Elizabeth Lake, the flesh and bones of a bear's victim—the park's sixth mauling fatality—were virtually consumed. Still, this type of behavior is rare, according to Dr. Charles Jonkel, who has studied grizzlies in and around Glacier. "In fact," said Jonkel, "statistically, bear maulings are rare, particularly when one considers the large number of people using the park's back country." Jonkel cautioned that bears are very much like humans. "Each and every one is an individual and, therefore, is unpredictable. This means hikers can't be sure of what to expect from a grizzly. If it sees a person in the distance, it usually will avoid him. But if the bear is surprised up close or if it sees a threat to itself or its cubs, it isn't going to cower. It didn't evolve that way."

Long-time Glacier hikers consider the chance of encountering a grizzly to be one of the risks they assume when they go into wild country. "But," said Glacier's Supervisory Research Biologist Clifford Martinka, "many other people aren't so tolerant. Most humans aren't able to mentally accept what you have to put up with when you have grizzlies around."

And so there are fewer and fewer grizzlies around for, as Martinka noted, "The grizzly is the type of animal that just can't take human pressure. And its problems today are essentially an indication of excessive human pressure—not just on the animal, but on its entire ecosystem."

The Natural World

GLACIER PARK MICRO-CLIMATE

by Bob Frauson

Right: Lightning storm in the Swiftcurrent area.

Facing page: Storm on St. Mary Lake.

Glacier National Park makes its own weather (micro-climate) due to its location straddling the Continental Divide. The predominant weather influence is the flow of moist, warm air from the Pacific, which loses heat as it rises over the west slope of the Continental Divide. Moisture is lost in the lower elevations as rain. Rain turns to snow as the air cools over the mountains. This same cool air then plunges down the eastern slope, gaining speed and warming to become chinook winds.

Cold fronts from the arctic flow down over the east front range from Siberia and Alaska, and through Alberta, forcing their way under the warmer Pacific air. Fronts may be visible as fog or clouds that form at the contact points between fronts and lightning even may occur from violent frontal clashes. Large arctic fronts tend to spill over the passes (Logan, Marias, etc.) and flow down into western valleys, filling them with cold air that is trapped under the warm, overriding air flowing east. This warm air plummets down the east slope as chinooks, and can create winds gusting in excess of 100 m.p.h. In such storms it is difficult to keep the rotating cups on anemometers, as they turn so fast that centrifugal force destroys them.

North winds, which are not winds as such, are the result of a constant pressure of chilling air moving south at from five to 10 m.p.h. Elk herds in winter tend to move into these north storms and have been known to move as far as eight miles in one night, leaving the boundaries of the park.

Cloud formations that signal weather changes are altocirrus clouds (mares' tails) moving in from the west. They usually precede storms from the west. Lenticular clouds (lens shaped) denote high winds from the west. These transform into chinook arches that can extend from horizon to horizon. In fall and winter, clouds can shroud the Continental Divide and its peaks for days on end. At other times, hat-like "cap clouds" settle on the major peaks.

It can snow in Glacier Park any month of the year. Sometimes snow closes Logan Pass as early as the second week in July. One can usually count on a snow storm on Logan Pass the third or fourth week of August, followed by a beautiful Indian summer. Snow that falls in the western valleys is likely to be moister than east slope snow. The rate of snowfall is a good indicator of avalanche danger. If it exceeds one inch per hour, winter travelers in mountainous terrain must beware. White-outs or ground blizzards can occur at any time, even many days after a snowfall, when there are strong winds and loose snow. Orientation is difficult under these conditions. A friend once described the difficulty of skiing in a white-out as "like skiing inside a ping-pong ball."

Temperature ranges are extreme and can change very rapidly. One may start on an afternoon cross-country ski trip from Hudson Bay Divide to St. Mary (seven-plus miles) in 25-below-zero weather, with beautiful gliding conditions, only to have the temperature rise to 45 above with rain. The snow becomes as sticky as mashed potatoes. The temperature can stay in the minus-25 to minus-35 temperature range for a week or so at a time. It sometimes dips to minus-50. Goats are good barometers of such weather fluctuations. Note their position on the mountain side: if they are high on the slopes, the weather will be good; when they are low, watch out!

Most of the large lakes in the park are very deep, so that a great deal of the water's cooling has to occur before ice can form on the surface. Lake McDonald seldom freezes over in the winter. Yet east-side lakes may freeze over by Thanksgiving. When the large lakes do freeze, one can hear constant booming in the valleys caused by cracking ice. Wind also affects a lake's ice

FREDERICK D. ATWOOD

CHARLES GURCHE

STAN OSOLINSKI

formation. On a calm, cool night the lake may freeze over. Then a wind might spring up to break the ice and send it grinding down the lake. Years ago, on just such an occasion, an elk herd went out onto St. Mary Lake on a night when the ice was not safe. Coyotes were out on the ice harassing the elk and the herd milled around in a small group. This concentration of weight caused the ice to break and about 40 elk drowned in a spot no larger than 30 feet square.

An Indian man by the name of Alanzo Skunk Cap told me his method of· forecasting a winter. He said to watch where the muskrats build their houses. If they are at the edge of the pond, it will be an easy winter. If the houses are in the middle of the pond, it will be a hard winter. Alanzo died a few years ago, but when I pass the ponds near his house I always watch where the muskrat houses are.

Tornadoes in Glacier Can't Be!?

In the spring of 1963, winds converged down the Swiftcurrent and Grinnell valleys starting a twister. The Many Glacier Hotel was the target for the swirling winds, which tore balconies and sections of roof from the old hotel. These winds continued east to the hotel parking area, where they picked up a large, old log garage that housed many tour buses in summer. The logs from the garage were scattered for about a half mile along the Cracker Lake Trail as far as the Governor's Pond. Power lines were downed in the area, starting small forest fires.

Surprise Flood in 1989

Historically, floods here occur in June. In 1989, heavy snows in the high country closed the Going-to-the-Sun Road over Logan Pass early in November. A freakish weather pattern hit the park with heavy rain for several days, melting snow at all elevations. Frost in the ground prevented water absorption, making for a heavy run-off. The Flathead River's North Fork and Middle Fork jumped to flood stage quickly, inundating the lowlands along the park boundaries. Railroad embankments were washed out. The Middle Fork was five feet above flood stage. Luckily, cool temperatures slowed the melt and the high waters subsided. Nearby Hungry Horse Reservoir on the South Fork of the Flathead River rose eight feet in a short period of time.

A break in the storm.

LIFE ZONES

by R.C. "Bert" Gildart

Here are profiles of plants and animals that typify the natural communities in which they are found. These are the "critters" and "green things" visitors often ask about that make Glacier the unusual natural treasure that it is. Certainly any of these living things is interesting in itself, but each can be seen as representative of those plants and animals subjected to common conditions in the habitat.

ALPINE COMMUNITY

The alpine community is perhaps the most spectacular, with its annual display of wildflowers. It is characterized by only a few species of trees, such as the arctic willow, birch and fir. A number of mammals, including the pika, marmot, wolverine and mountain goat, have made interesting adaptations to this harshest of parkland environments. Deer use this area as a summer home.

Ptarmigan Hard, wind-blown snow comes early in the high peaks of the Rocky Mountain range. It drives the elk down into the low country; it covers the boulder-strewn home of the mouse-like pika; and it sends the powerful grizzly bear scurrying to its den for a long winter's nap. In fact, the rugged alpine country forces just about every type of creature to leave or hide. But always there remains a beautiful little one-pound bird—the ptarmigan.

I first met this strange bird while cross-country skiing with a ranger friend in Glacier National Park. The temperature was five degrees below zero and the wind was howling across the vast treeless flat. Both of us were bundled in heavy down coats, warm leather mittens and thick wooly long johns. All around us the snowy world seemed a mighty deserted place. But suddenly, not more than a half dozen paces away, were six balls of puffed-up feathers. They were pure white, as white as the snow over which we traveled. It seemed a miracle that we had not passed them by. Perhaps the flutter of their wings as they scooted deeper into the snow attracted our attention or maybe it was the black of their eyes and beaks that contrasted so sharply with the endless snow. We wanted a better look and so we moved closer, trying not to startle them. But we need not have worried; fear was not part of their nature, and they only returned our stares as if to say, "Any creature out in this weather must be just another ptarmigan."

Ptarmigans are unusual birds. So well have they learned to live with their environment that for years we humans have been trying to copy their survival

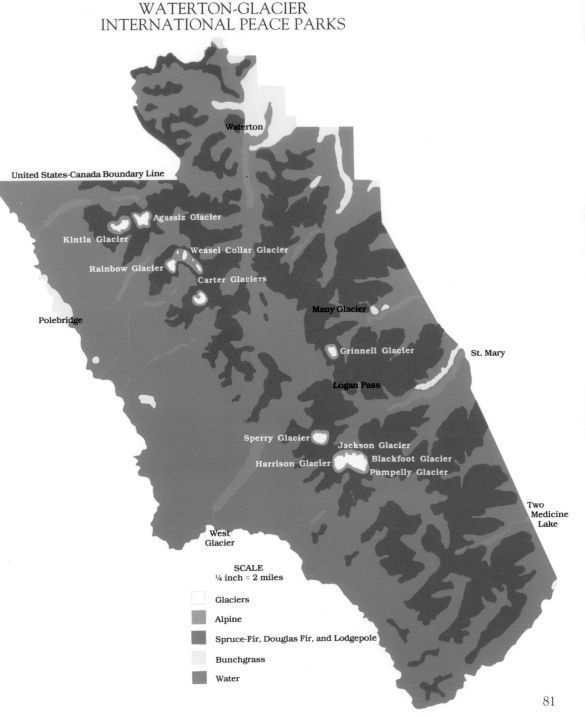

WATERTON-GLACIER
INTERNATIONAL PEACE PARKS

Waterton

United States-Canada Boundary Line

Agassiz Glacier

Kintla Glacier

Weasel Collar Glacier

Rainbow Glacier

Carter Glaciers

Polebridge

Many Glacier

Grinnell Glacier

St. Mary

Logan Pass

Sperry Glacier

Jackson Glacier

Blackfoot Glacier

Harrison Glacier

Pumpelly Glacier

West Glacier

Two Medicine Lake

SCALE
¼ inch = 2 miles

Glaciers
Alpine
Spruce-Fir, Douglas Fir, and Lodgepole
Bunchgrass
Water

81

Above left: *Ptarmigans wearing winter plumage.*

Above right: *Ptarmigan in its summer camouflage.*

Right: *Wolverine on the hunt.*

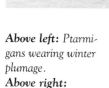

WERNER STEBNER

82

techniques. But thinking back now on those six birds "bathing" in the snow sends a chill through me, and I'll have to admit that I question how far we have come toward mastering their skills.

If you have heard of the ptarmigan, you probably thought it a resident of the Arctic or Alaskan tundra. But in some mountain regions of our western states, one of the three Northern American ptarmigans, the white-tailed, often is found.

The ptarmigan is a close relative of the grouse. The white-tailed ptarmigan has the scientific name *Lagopus leucurus*. In simple translation of Latin its first name, *Lagopus*, means "rabbit foot." During the winter all ptarmigans grow long stiff feathers over their feet. Their feet do look a lot like rabbit feet. They can walk right on top of soft, fluffy snow where I, even on my snowshoes or skis, often sink deep. On their own "snowshoes," ptarmigans easily make their way in search of willows, birches and alders that usually have twigs sticking up above the snow.

Ptarmigan chicks are born in June in the arctic-alpine community, where it is still very cold. Unlike many other birds, ptarmigans are born already covered with soft, warm feathers. And a baby ptarmigan is up scratching around in just an hour. One week later, it is testing its wings.

Even with this head start, the life of a ptarmigan chick is not such an easy one. It must be on the lookout for such predators as the hawk, weasel and wolverine and other inhabitants of the arctic alpine community. Fortunately, nature has provided a camouflage for all seasons. In summer the feathers of young and adults alike are a blend of brown and white. So well do they fit in with the rocks and boulders that an occasional hiker is seriously startled when a lichen-covered "rock" sails off into the blue, cackling and beating its wings as it goes.

To me the most beautiful coloration occurs in the winter, when the white-tailed ptarmigan is all white. Its close relatives, the willow and rock ptarmigan, however, retain small areas of black. For years biologists thought the gradual replacement of feathers and the seasonal changes in color were regulated by differences in temperature. Carefully controlled laboratory experiments, however, have shown that it is the seasonal changes in day length that regulate the color of the ptarmigan.

Feathers not only help the ptarmigan blend with its surroundings but also provide excellent protection from the cold. During the winter, the ptarmigan fluffs up its feathers, creating "dead" air spaces that help trap the heat produced by its body. We do much the same thing by shaking quilts and sleeping bags that are filled with feathers.

The ptarmigan conserves heat by taking advantage of the insulating qualities of the snow. Ptarmigans make their caves by diving into the snow and scratching out a hollow, or by pressing their bodies into the soft powder and then merely letting the wind pack drifts of snow around them. Outside these snow "rooms" the wind may be 40 degrees below zero, but inside it is relatively calm and cozy.

If the snow is soft, ptarmigans can wander around underneath it, where they may feed on buried twigs. Sometimes, if snow crusts on top, the birds become trapped in ice chambers where they may die. A friend of mine once heard such an unfortunate bird clucking softly beneath him under an icy crust of snow. Kneeling down, he took the tip of his ski pole and carefully chipped away at the ice. Suddenly, with a furious beat of its wings, the trapped bird broke into the air and sailed away on a gust of wind. "Maybe we'll see that one again," said my surprised friend. That happy thought sent us sliding off with the same wind that had taken our freedom-bound ptarmigan.

Above: *Marmot near Gunsight Pass.*
Left: *A pika busy with its harvesting.*

Rocky Mountain Big Horn Sheep

Rocky Mountain bighorn sheep are almost synonymous with Glacier Park to many visitors, because of their visibility in the highly-visited area of Many Glacier. In summer above the historic Many Glacier Hotel, and at other spots such as Haystack Butte, bands of sheep can be seen in seeming peace. But in the mating season of autumn, Many Glacier Valley resounds with cracking blows of horns as males endure annual dominance battles.

Mountain Goat

As with the bighorn sheep, there are a few special places where the mountain goat is frequently sought and photographed.

Gunsight Pass is such a place. The classic Glacier Park photo of mountain goats lounging on a rocky outcrop with a jewel of a lake hundreds of feet below likely was taken at Gunsight Pass, showing Lake Ellen Wilson in the background. Goats exist throughout the park, but usually are not so easy to find, choosing to live in an environment so remote that they fear little from predators, but suffer instead from the elements and dangers of their craggy homesteads.

Left: Bighorn ewe. **Above:** Bighorn ram. **Facing page:** Mountain goat.

LEE KAISER

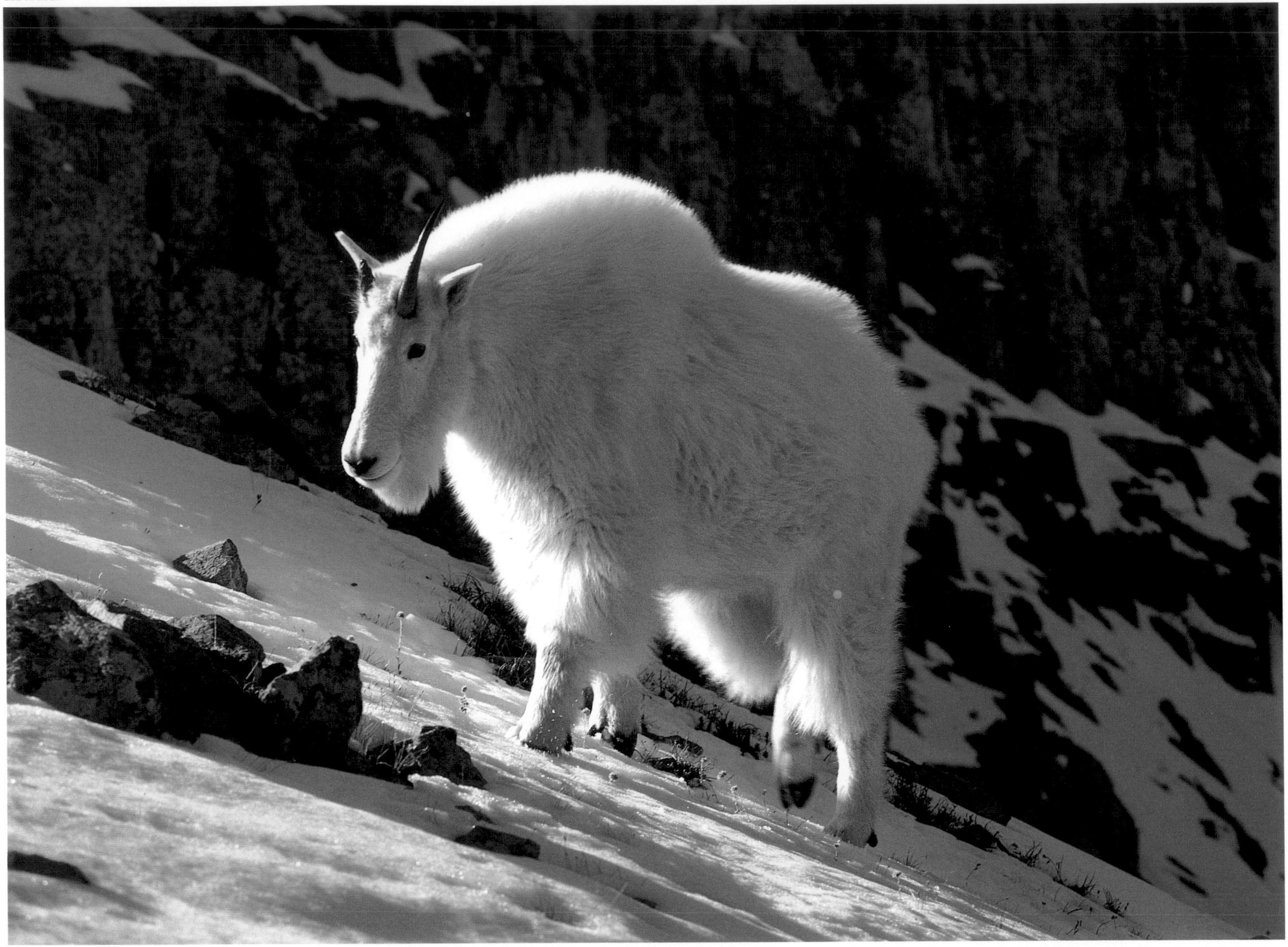

PAT O'HARA

LEFT: WERNER STEBNER; BELOW: BRECK P. KENT

SPRUCE–FIR
AND DOUGLAS FIR

These two communities are treated together as they are interspersed with one another from about 4,000 to 7,000 feet. Also, only a few species of mammals prefer one of these areas over the other. Soil conditions and slope direction are two of the factors that determine which of the two communities dominates a certain site. Look for Douglas fir on southerly slopes and spruce and fir on the north-facing slopes. These communities are home for furbearers and many of the large mammals.

Above left: *Bobcat.*
Above right: *Mountain lion.*
Left: *Red fox.*

Facing page: *Lower Two Medicine Lake.*

WERNER STEBNER

Male spruce grouse.

female and proclaims his territorial rights with his "drumming." With the female in attendance, the male flies to the top of a tall spruce, performing an aerial display of wing beats and color patches.

There are several variations of the spruce grouse's drumming procedure. Instead of flying out of the top of the tree as do other grouse, the male may fly from the limb of one tree to the limb of a nearby tree, fluttering his wings and drumming as he goes. Descending to the ground, he may pass back and forth from tree to tree, performing all the way down. At other times, the male may fly repeatedly straight up in the air without landing in any tree, displaying while he is descending.

Yet another variation has been recorded where the spruce grouse flies and hops up an inclined tree, drumming as it goes. Nearing the thicker branches at the top of the tree, the grouse flies to the ground, only to start up again.

When the male spruce grouse is on the ground, he displays and struts for the female like a miniature tom turkey. His feathers are ruffled so that they stand on end; the head is held up and back. The tail, the grouse's glory, is fanned out to its very fullest and raised almost vertically. Hikers encountering a male spruce grouse spreading its splendid glistening tail in a sunlit opening among the pines will know they have entered the depths of the park.

The spruce grouse is well named, for it prefers to live in and around spruce trees, whose needles provide one of its staple foods. Other requirements are abundant huckleberry plants, insects for the young, a sparse ground covering and tree groves with openings of a few hundred square feet. A spruce grouse could ask for little more in life, except perhaps a little peace and quiet.

What do spruce grouse contribute to the overall welfare of the forest? Because spruce trees give up some of their needles to spruce grouse, their overall growth might be infinitesimally faster without the grouse. Huckleberries might produce better without spruce grouse removing their leaves and flowers, but fruits were meant to be eaten so that their seeds may be dispersed after passing through animals' digestive systems. So spruce grouse probably help huckleberries more than they hurt them.

In some small way spruce grouse may help increase the turnover rate of nutrients in their habitat, and thereby increase the amount of life their surroundings can support. When they eat conifer needles, for example, spruce grouse turn over the nutrients in the food chain in four ways: back into the soil in the form of droppings or through the decay of spruce grouse carcasses, in the excretion of an animal that has eaten a spruce grouse, or through decay of such a predator's carcass. In some favorite winter haunts spruce grouse droppings may be so abundant that they increase plant growth.

The spruce grouse, as a vegetarian, concentrates and converts plant material into protein and fats of its body. Other inhabitants or visitors of the spruce–fur community, such as the goshawk, great horned owl, red fox and coyote are all somewhat better off for the presence of the spruce grouse, but none of those predators depends primarily on the spruce grouse as a source of protein. Thus it seems that the role of the spruce grouse in the broad scheme of life is a minor one, and that the world could go on without it. Still, that the "fool hen" has not yet learned to fear man means there are places that yet retain the vestiges of wildness.

Spruce Grouse

Hikers passing through the spruce–fir community of Glacier Park often are surprised by a mottled dark gray or brown bird with a conspicuous black face, throat, and chest patch or bib—which demonstrates absolutely no fear of the hikers' approach. Upon seeing the bird, hikers are further surprised to find that if they walk toward it, the bird may do nothing more than circle a nearby tree. If charged, the bird may fly to an overhanging branch, but seldom will it fly away, although it does possess excellent powers of flight. Spruce grouse apparently feel so secure in the depths of their surroundings that some don't even feel intimidated when approached to within arm's length. There are documented cases of people who have reached out and plucked the bird off its perch. Because of this total lack of fear, this wilderness grouse has earned the name "fool hen."

Other than a lack of fear, the ritualistic courtship of the spruce grouse is probably the bird's most interesting feature. These displays can be seen in Glacier's North Fork country in April. The male spruce grouse displays for the

Above left: *Silky lupine.*
Above: *Elk.*
Left: *Short-tail weasel.*

LODGEPOLE–LARCH COMMUNITY

This area indicates frequent and severe burning and is particularly noticeable along Camas Creek Road and in the Apgar region. It is a successional community that will ultimately lead to spruce–fir or cedar–hemlock communities. Elk are common in this area.

Tamarack

Tamaracks, as they have since the beginning of tamaracks, change color each fall and blaze like bronze flames. When they do, people inevitably look at the species—intermingled with the green of its common associate, the lodgepole pine—and wonder why the hillside is full of dying trees.

Tamaracks are one of the exceptions to the rule that members of the family *Pinacea* retain their leaves or needles. Another exception is the bald cypress that proliferates in the Everglades of Florida. Tamaracks, then, are properly designated as deciduous conifers; they shed their needles in the fall and stand naked through the winter. But before the needles fall, they turn the most beautiful bronze-tan color imaginable. Next spring the tamaracks will come to blossom: the female flowers with scarlet scales and the male flowers bright yellow, tiny blossoms with delicate colors that seem almost out of place. A few weeks later they will shimmer with new light-green needles.

New spring needles help differentiate them from those of the other needled trees. The needles are from one to two inches in length and occur in bundles of about 15 to 30, growing along the length of the small branchlets. The cones are small, yellowish-brown, about an inch long, and have thin, flexible scales.

Such spring delicacy could be achieved only by a tree as tough and sturdy as a tamarack, which grows farther north than any other tree in North America. Its finest groves are to be found north of the Great Lakes. There it thrives in the boglands, but in the northern Rockies it grows on rocky ridges too.

Tamaracks are also known as hackmatack and larch, and in most areas of Montana it is called buckskin, possibly because of the bright tan color of its bark.

Western larch is a prolific seeder and is a close competitor of the lodgepole pine in seeding burned-over areas. The tall, thick-barked mature larches often withstand the heat of forest fires, and, if soil conditions are favorable, will seed heavily in the vicinity of the surviving trees. This can be seen in several places on the western side of the park, notably the northwestern side of Quartz Ridge near the foot of Bowman Lake.

Tamaracks often are sought out by the firewood gatherers in the fall. Wood from dead buckskins splits easily, readily creating a cheery glow in the hearth, and providing warmth on a cold Montana evening. Weathered buckskins also provide sites for cavity-nesting birds: one old spiraling tamarack was found to be a home for 12 species of birds and 20 nesting pairs. Glacier National Park naturalist, Dr. Riley McClellan, recommended several years ago to Forest Service personnel that a few snags, such as tamarack buckskins, be marked and left standing until toppled by wind and erosion. Standing dead trees provide ecological harmony to the forest and create warmth and security for many of our avian migrants that inhabit the lodgepole–larch community.

Left: *Overgrowth heals the scars of 1967's lightning-caused Glacier Wall fire.*

Facing page: *Western larch in autumn foliage.*

CEDAR–HEMLOCK COMMUNITY

A rather small area confined to the McDonald drainage of Glacier National Park and dependent upon large quantities of moisture, this community extends from 3,100 feet to about 4,000 feet. Whitetail deer, moose and red squirrels occasionally are seen here.

Above: Moose.
Far left: *Paper birch and Western red cedars along Lake McDonald.*
Left: *Whitetail bucks in velvet.*

Facing page, left: *The sculptured walls of Avalanche Gorge demonstrate Avalanche Creek's power before it empties into Lake McDonald.* **Right:** *Skunk cabbage in the spring.*

Cedar and Hemlock

The red cedar in Glacier is restricted primarily to an area between Avalanche Campground and the shoreline bordering the upper end of McDonald Lake. Here, a few trees reach great dimensions, with a few specimens 220 feet tall and seven feet in diameter. Prior to 1910, this community extended over a larger area, but the intense fires of that season eliminated even this thick-barked tree.

The McDonald Valley is ideal for the red cedar's growth. In this part of the park, rain and snow are abundant and the humidity is relatively high. Two ridges, Howe and Snyder, flank the valley, and keep the McDonald drainage fairly cool.

Western red cedar is not important to wildlife, except possibly to provide cover for the deer, squirrels, grouse and smaller birds that frequent the area. The seeds of red cedars often are bypassed in preference to the larger cones of nearby conifers.

Cedar was used extensively by Indians over much of the northwest. The trunk was used for canoes and lodges, while the strong, tough inner bark became baskets.

Cedars begin their life cycle in mid-April by producing flowers. As the season progresses, the fruits or cones mature and, in late August, seeds are shed. These slow-growing trees begin to produce flowers and fruits at about 20 years of age, but do not produce their peak seed crops until reaching 70 to 80. Then they continue to produce seeds for 100 to 200 more years. As with other species of cedar, they produce a heavy seed crop about every three years.

Growing in close association with the red cedar is the western hemlock, confined to the same area defined by climatic and topographic conditions. Frequently the two species are confused. To differentiate between them, look at the needles. Those of the cedar are fern-like and may overlap one another; those of the hemlock are blunt. Also look at the tips of two mature specimens. On the western hemlock, the tip droops to form a "leader," while the tip of the cedar stands erect.

Above: *Columbia ground squirrel young at play.*
Far left: *Shooting star.*
Left: *Coyote.*

Facing page: *Alder (left) and Western red cedar along the "Trail of the Cedars" above Lake McDonald near Avalanche Creek.*

BUNCHGRASS COMMUNITY

Although scattered sites of bunchgrass and its associated vegetation range up to 6,000 feet, this community generally is confined to elevations below 5,000 feet. East of the Continental Divide, this community can be recognized by its prairie-like appearance and stands of cottonwood and aspen. Areas between St. Mary and Rising Sun along the Going-to-the-Sun Road are typical of the bunchgrass community. Some of the mammals that historically inhabited this area are the bison, muskrat, badger, elk and coyote.

JEFF GNASS

Annuals and Perennials

For nine to 10 months they lie dormant: plants that show no flowering life and exist only as seeds, roots, tubers or underground stems. Should you dig one up and look at it all covered with mud, it would appear lifeless; but on the 10th or 11th month, transitions begin to occur. Beginning to emerge are the tiny structures known as epicotyls, hypocotyls and cotyledons. These are the predecessors of leaves, roots and the areas of nutrition.

By the end of the 10th month, or around the middle of June, snows have receded, and the duration of daily sunshine is at its greatest. Then these tiny structures begin shooting upward, as much as an inch a day in some species.

By the end of July, tiny buds begin to unfurl. And soon these plants, which for a time were drab and difficult to identify, sparkle and assume unique identities. They bounce in the wind, roll across the plains, and tingle as morning zephyrs waft across their faces. For a brief moment, when measured against the course of a year, they add a multiplicity of colors to the prairie and foothills of the parks.

Yarrow, fleabane, potentilla, cinquefoil, spirea, crazyweed and lupine are a few of the 1,000 or so species growing in the park. A large percentage of these may be seen in the park's bunchgrass community commingling to form this colorful pageantry.

Many of these plants are annuals, or species that produce seeds that must start anew each year. By comparison, perennials sprout each year from roots and produce an annual growth of seeds.

All of the emerging plants serve a vital function in the overall ecological picture. The beneficial effects of some, however, are more readily recognized. Wild geranium is a major food item for elk and deer in spring and summer. At times, black and grizzly bears also consume this plant. It may be recognized by its five rose-purple petals, each of which measures about a half inch across. Stems, leaves and some flower parts are covered with sticky, glandular hairs.

Cinquefoil, which blooms throughout the summer, is used by scientists as an indicator plant. If this plant is being browsed, wildlife biologists know the range is being overgrazed. Because it has five petals and five sepals, it is classified as a rose, although it has no thorns.

Yarrow, a plant that produces a white flower, is used medicinally as a stimulant and as a tonic. Indians were familiar with its medicinal applications ages ago. The species' generic name, *Achillea*, comes from the Greek hero Achilles, supposed to have used yarrow to heal his wounded warriors after the siege of Troy.

In some years, the density of the flowers is greater than in other years. Heavy spring rains followed by abundant sunshine may be responsible for this profusion. During these times, colors of every hue run up one coulee and down another—running beyond the limits of the imagination as they merge with the sapphire of St. Mary Lake and the aqua of the eastern skies.

WILF SCHURIG

STAN OSOLINSKI

NEAL & MARY JANE MISHLER

Above: *Goldenrod.*
Above left: *Wood lily.*
Left: *Sticky geranium.*

Facing page: *September color in the Glacier ecosystem; Divide Mountain on the horizon.*

TRIPLE DIVIDE

Of all the mountains in Glacier National Park, Triple Divide Peak is one of the most significant. Rising to an elevation of 8,020 feet, it easily can be reached by leaving the campground in Cut Bank Valley where a trail leads for approximately eight miles to Triple Divide Pass. From here an hour-long scramble will take you to the summit. The easiest route up the mountain leads directly from the pass, and is marked by rock cairns.

From its apex, waters drain down Atlantic Creek, eventually to reach the Gulf of Mexico. Across the ridge to the left, water flows southwest down Pacific Creek ultimately to mingle with the blue Pacific at the mouth of the Columbia River. To the right, on the other side of the pass, water drains from this peak down Hudson Bay Creek in its course to Hudson Bay. No other peak in North America has drainage into three seas so distant and through water courses as long as the three river systems: the Missouri-Mississippi, the Columbia and the Saskatchewan-Nelson. Here is the meeting of the three major divides of North America; the Atlantic-Pacific, the Pacific-Hudson Bay, and the Hudson Bay-Atlantic. But for all of its significance, Triple Divide Peak is not high, since it is only a spur of Norris Mountain to the northwest.

Left: *Looking southwest along the Cut Bank drainage. The flat-topped peaks, near left, are Mad Wolf Mountain and (with snowfield) Bad Marriage Mountain.*

Facing page: *Whitetail fawn.*

JOHN REDDY

Influencing the 1990s

ALAN & SANDY CAREY

The Wolves Return

Wolves were once an integral part of the Glacier National Park ecosystem. But in the early 1920s, aggressive hunting and a park philosophy that promoted the preservation of prey species contrived to eliminate predators. Rangers hunted wolves, and trapped, poisoned and shot other meat eaters such as wolverines, coyotes and bears. Today, park officials recognize the importance of predators.

The park supports a number of biological concepts once viewed as taboo. The result is that bold management actions are accommodating fire, pine beetle infestations and other natural occurrences. Aggressive actions toward humans by grizzly bears in defense of young or of a food source are tolerated. Managers are trying to define the park's role in the surrounding ecosystem and at the same time are attempting to bring the good news of an enlightened biological era to the 2 million visitors who enter the park each year.

The return of the wolf to Glacier may be the challenge of the era.

Except for occasional sightings of isolated wolves, the species was absent from Glacier National Park until 1982, when a female gave birth to a litter just north of the park in British Columbia. Their presence excited the scientific community, and attempts were made to follow the animals' activities. First, scientists captured several animals and fitted them with radio collars. Then they began documenting wolf movements. Dens were located and a great deal of information emerged.

Biologists learned that the wolves called the North and South Camas Pack ranged through the park and north into Canada. Two other packs, known as the Spruce and Headwater packs, generally named after the area they roam, commonly stay to the north and west in British Columbia.

Wolves have been sighted in a variety of park areas. Fifty-one sightings were recorded in the park in 1993, which represents a 16 percent increase in the wolf population since the 1992 count. Wolves also were documented in other northwestern Montana areas, and sighted on no fewer than 150 occasions by the mid-1990s. Interestingly, the wolves in the Park thrived without court battles, political wars, or television cameras. Quite the opposite was true in 1995, the eve of the return of wolves to Yellowstone National Park through a massive transplant effort, where wolves were either cursed and vilified ,or loved and eulogized.

Biologists from the park and from the U.S. Fish and Wildlife Service, sharing ranchers' concern about livestock predation, attempted to relocate a pack of wolves away from a farm area and into the park in September of 1989. Three of the four pack members did not survive the transplant attempt, but much was learned in the effort. The surviving wolf traveled over mountains and valleys, swam the Hungry Horse Reservoir, and eventually established a territory in the Mission Mountains near Seeley Lake, more than 50 miles away.

Gray wolf.

Bears & Humans

Today's park staff aggressively seeks information about bears. All park staff and visitors are encouraged to report bear sightings. These documented sightings add to the storehouse of knowledge about bears, and help the National Park Service manage bears.

The area's bear population reached a low point about 1915, during the heyday of sheep ranching. Sheepherders and ranchers shot virtually any bear they saw, and park managers encouraged rangers to kill bears.

Today, Glacier's biologists believe grizzly bear numbers average 200, or about one grizzly for every eight square miles. In 1994, visitors reported seeing 2,075 bears and, in 1993, 1,694. Both figures are less than in 1989, when visitors reported a record number of 2,935 bears. More than half of the sightings were reported as grizzlies.

Unfortunately, not all bear sightings and encounters end peacefully. Bears began killing in 1967 when two girls were fatally mauled in one night in two areas separated by great distance. More recently, in 1992, near Granite Park Chalet (where on of the 1967 maulings occurred), a grizzly with two cubs killed a photographer who was apparently hiking around a blind corner when he surprised the bears. This incident raised the park's total of fatal maulings to nine. The sow must have attacked immediately, killing the man. Several hours later another hiker found the victim and departed for help. The bears then returned to feed on the body, creating some of the park's most lurid bear headlines. Following an intensive hunt, rangers killed the family unit for fear a patter of human–bear association had been established.

Prior to that, Glacier's grizzlies had killed two people in 1987. One of these deaths was the result of a photographer aggressively pursuing a sow with cubs near elk Mountain not far from West Glacier along the Middle Fork of the Flathead River. That mauling also created headlines, but one sympathetic toward the bear. The bear wasn't destroyed. Other fatal maulings have occurred at Many Glacier, St. Mary, and Elizabeth Lake. Non-fatal maulings have occurred throughout the Park and now number about 60.

Despite the maulings, statistically, the level of risk is an acceptable one. In 1994, the number of back-country campers reached its highest level ever, approaching 30,600. Even with the high usage, the number of bear encounters was down, a testimony to good park management.

Most maulings involve females with cubs. In 1989, this was the case for two incidents injuring three people. Two backpackers surprised a female with cubs near Cracker Lake in Many Glacier Valley; separately, another female with two cubs attacked and bit a man on the leg near Granite Park Chalet. Park scientists also have documented an increase in maulings by subadult bears.

Because grizzlies are more prone to attack than are black bears, wildlife managers today seek to learn to differentiate between the species from their droppings. Sophisticated but expensive techniques now being developed permit such analysis. For example, bile from black bears and grizzly bears differs chemically. By using high-tech laboratory procedures to examine bear droppings, differences in the bile can be determined and the species identified.

Repeated appearances by the same bear in an area of high human concentration confirm that the animal has become habituated to the presence of people or conditioned to their food. Habituation means that a bear has lost its normal fear of people and presents a potentially dangerous situation. Glacier's evolving Bear Management Program provides written guidelines how such bears must be handled. In the broadest sense, the guidelines are extraordinarily clear-cut: Keep grizzlies and people separated!

The park accomplished this mandate in several different ways. First, management insists on a pack-in pack-out policy. It also provides food storage facilities at all 62 back-country camp grounds, which together provide 208 sites.

Second, the park uses trail closures. From experience, biologists know that when snow and ice melts, opening the avalanche chutes in areas such as Avalanche Lake, bears will be there, attracted by delectable glacier lily bulbs. Biologists also know that, as the season progresses, bears turn to huckleberry-rich sites on Apgar Mountain. At the appropriate times, these areas are closed to people annually. Other areas are closed on a case-by-case basis. In a typical year, trail closures average about 34, all of them temporary.

The last method of separation is referred to as a preemptive move. Bears that have become habituated to the presence of humans and frequent developed areas are moved before they create problems. Those that return may be killed if suitable but more remote locations cannot be found. But usually no one wants a problem bear transplated to their area.

People often create problem bears by feeding them directly or indirectly. As a result, rangers issue citations that carry stiff fines for the violation of a rule that should be clear: "Don't feed the animals."

Regardless of the improved management record, bear–human encounters do occur. For those times, bear authorities recommend that hikers include as standard gear a cayenne pepper spray, which can be legally carried in the park. When used appropriately, the results have been effective, although managers warn that hikers carrying pepper spray should not throw caution to the wind, because nothing—no matter how effective—ever works 100 percent of the time.

Regardless of the improved management record, bear–human encounters do occur. For those times, bear authorities recommend that hikers include as standard gear a cayenne pepper spray, which can be legally carried in the park. When used appropriately, the results have been effective, although managers warn that hikers carrying pepper spray should not throw caution to the wind, because nothing—no matter how effective—ever works 100 percent of the time.

The Ecosystem View

Not only have Glacier personnel assumed a front role in grizzly bear management, but also they have established themselves as leaders in confronting issues that may not be within their immediate jurisdiction. Words such as ecosystem now crop up regularly, and rightfully so, for Glacier National Park is not an island, and management decisions made by other agencies significantly affect the park itself.

One important area of the Glacier ecosystem is the Badger-Two Medicine. This extraordinary piece of land is flanked on the south by the Bob Marshall Wilderness Area, on the east by the Blackfeet Indian Reservation, and on the north by Glacier National Park proper.

In 1989, Glacier's superintendent summarized the park's position: The Badger-Two Medicine provides an important linkage of "habitat and travel corridors for wildlife that spends a portion of each year in the park." Implicit in his statement was the conviction that the Badger should be managed as a wilderness area, one that could have a significant influence on the ecosystem's wildlife.

The Forest Service administers the Badger, but its policies are not always popular with conservationists, Native Americans or the National Park Service. In a 1989 Environmental Impact Statement, the Forest Service recommended construction of new roads in the Badger, to accommodate the heavy equipment of oil companies.

The battle seems destined to persist, though Blackfeet Indians have used the Badger in traditional religious practices from time immemorial. Blackfeet Indian spokesmen applauded the park's ecosystem approach. Said Galen Bullshoe "...our grandfathers went up in the Badger-Two Medicine to fast and sweat. Their spirits are still up there. The elk herds that I hunt up by Goat Mountain would leave if they drilled up there."

In 1977, UNESCO designated Glacier as a World Biosphere Reserve. This recognized the value of Glacier National Park's ecological resources for both conservation and scientific work. Such a designation means that park managers must maintain watchful eyes toward surrounding development. Oil and gas exploration threaten wildlife, quietness, solitude and water quality, and the park's naturally functioning ecosystems.

Glacier may also assume a role in another ecosystem concept entitled the "Crown of the Continent project," referring to the area extending from south of the Bob Marshall Wilderness through Glacier National Park and terminating just north of Waterton National Park. Though managers suggested construction of a research facility, funds have not been available. Nevertheless, the philosophy remains, which expresses the hope that managers from the various land management agencies will work together to monitor and educate and facilitate policy discussions regarding a Crown of hte Continent Ecosystem approach.

Proposed development along the North Fork of the Flathead River long has been another area of concern. In 1989, however, conservationists appeared victorious over developers for the first time in decades.

That year, the International Joint Commission (IJC) recommended that an open-pit coal mine proposal for north of the international border not be approved by the British Columbia government. (Established by the 1909 Boundary Waters Treaty, the commission includes three representatives chosen by Canada's prime minister and three named by the U.S. president.) The open-pit coal mine, proposed by Toronto-based Sage Creek Ltd., would have been located at the confluence of Cabin and Howell creeks in British Columbia approximately six miles north of the U.S. border. The mine would have impacted the North Fork drainage, and so the proposal required four years of study by the IJC. Along with recommending against that particular project, the commission further recommended that the two nations work together to develop management strategies to benefit the upper Flathead River basin.

Despite general agreement reached by the two countries, other companies proposed in 1995 several projects that would have almost the same impact on water quality as that proposed by Sage Creek Ltd. For conservationists and for fishery managers the stakes are high, for at risk is the future of one of nature's great species, the Dolly Varden (bull trout). Ground water flowing from the several proposed mine sites feeding into the North Fork could introduce toxic levels of nitrogenous compounds, changing river temperatures and altering oxygen levels. Such modifications would drastically alter the North Fork, a prime spawning area for Dolly Varden. Glacier considers the species to be a genetically unique resource and because other areas of the state containing Dolly Varden have been compromised, park management attempts an aggressive preservation role.

One mountain threat to Glacier's tranquillity and possibly its wildlife is the increased number of low-flying aircraft. Once, such flights were manageable because commercial helicopter pilots tended to work park managers. Several years ago, much of a pilot's summer pay was derived from park service contracts, involving search and rescue. In 1994, another commercial venture opened, bringing the number of commercial helicopters operating directly in the Park to three. In addition, there are a number of fixed-wing aircraft operators who also buzz the park. In addition to detracting from the wilderness qualities of Glacier, research indicates wildlife may be adversely affected. In an effort to mitigate the disturbance of aircraft, the Park has requested pilots limit sight-seeing flights to above 2,000 feet. Some pilots have ignored the request, descending to the 500-foot level—as this writer has observed! Although the 500-foot level is accepted by the Federal Aviation Administration, the level is not compatible with quality Park visitation. As a result, many visitors have objected by writing their congressmen.

One other area of great concern is the restored use of the Park's two chalets, specifically Granite Park Chalet and Sperry Chalet. For decades, the chalets eased the difficulty of backpacking through Glacier. But increased health concerns forced their closure, and now, although plans exist that would render the chalets environmentally acceptable, the millions of dollars required for such construction don't exist. Because the U.S. government has listed them as National Historic Landmarks, one day their sewage and water facilities will be improved. The question that remains is, when? Most would like to see them restored.

Red Bench Fire of 1988

On September 7, 1988, a fire started by lightning in the adjacent Flathead National Forest crossed the river into Glacier National Park and eventually burned a total of 27,000 acres. Although it did not attract the media attention that the Yellowstone National Park fires of the same year received, this fire was extensive. Called the Red Bench Fire, it destroyed 28 dwellings and and several outbuildings, including several historic structures built in the 1920s at Polebridge. It collapsed the bridge over the North Fork of the Flathead River, warping its steel girders as a firestorm erupted.

An interagency team was formed to fight the fire. During the height of the fire, 1,600 firefighters were actively engaged in battling the inferno. Fourteen firefighters were injured, mostly by falling snags. One man on the national forest side of the fire was killed when a burned tree silently fell and struck a group of five firefighters waiting for a ride back to base camp.

Experts agreed that prevailing conditions minimized the chances of stopping the fires of 1988 throughout the West. Red Bench was no exception. Fanned by 40-miles-per-hour winds, within hours it burned hundreds of acres.

When the smoke cleared, there was one pleasant surprise: The historic Polebridge Ranger Station, thought to have been swept away by fire, remained intact, as did several other buildings in the fire area.

To restore cultural features, mitigate damage caused by suppression efforts and study the effects of the fire on the animals and plants of the area, the park received $1.1 million. This money was to fund a number of projects including reconstruction of barns, seasonal housing and back-country trails, removal of hazardous trees, replacement of lost or damaged vehicles, and repair of areas marred by bulldozers or fire lines. Natural areas altered by the fire were left for nature's healing.

Although many viewed the Red Bench Fire as a tragedy, park managers consider lightning-started fires to be natural events. Gary Gregory, a resource management specialist, said, "The forest will burn, but it is a natural process that is part of the way that forests stay healthy. Fire creates much of the diversity that makes the park so interesting." As a result of this philosophy, fires such as the 8,000-acre Howling Creek Fire of 1994 were permitted to burn, although it was closely monitored.

Fires, according to park managers, are integral parts of any natural area. New forests and rejuvenated grasslands provide their own arrays of flora and fauna. Only months after a fire, lodgepole pine seedlings begin popping up, as do a variety of forbs and shrubs. These species pave the way for others in the natural succession of the forest, and provide ever-changing habitat for wildlife.

According to park managers, man has just begin to realize the importance of fire as a natural part of the forest ecosystem. Years of fire suppression may have contributed to the conditions that fueled the fires of 1988. As managers learn more about fire, they hope to better manage natural resources.

The burned areas are readily visible to visitors traveling to Polebridge and proceeding either north toward Kintla Lake or east to Bowman Lake. Along either route, you will encounter trails that lead right into burned areas.

DIANE ENSIGN

The Quartz Creek Trail, for example, is located about four miles south of Polebridge. The Quartz Lake Trail begins at Bowman Lake, crossing Quartz Ridge to Quartz Lake. Along the trails or the roads of the North Fork, you will see a forest's resilience in the wake of forest fire.

Overleaf: *Between Logging Creek and Bowman Lake.*

Smoke-filtered sun glares down on burned trees during the Red Bench Fire.

*You cannot
improve it.
The ages have
been at work
on it, and
man can only
mar it.*

Theodore
Roosevelt